# PONDERINGS OF A PPC PROFESSIONAL

### A Collection of Philosophical, Yet Practical, Observations to Help You Win at Pay-Per-Click Marketing

## Kirk Williams

ZATOWorks

ebook ISBN: 9780578778488
paperback ISBN: 9780578770192

ZATOWorks Publishing
Cover design by: aksaramantra on 99Designs.com

Printed in the United States of America

*Not all who ponder are lost.*

# Dedication

*To my parents and parents in-law: your support in my life has made me who I am, and I am thankful daily for each of the four of you and your impact on my business and personal life.*

*To my ZATO team members, past, present, and future: Your questions and at times, necessary push-back on my crazy ideas, make me a better PPCer and person. Never stop.*

*To my children, the BHive: You are the pride of my life, my greatest accomplishment. Keep serving Jesus, loving life, laughing, working hard, and above all and most importantly, never lose your father's love of BBQ.*

*To my wife, Elise: I couldn't do life without you. Thank you for putting up with me, my foibles, quibbles, and quirks. We make a pretty darn good team, and I look forward to the decades we have left together.*

# Praise For Ponderings:

*"Kirk drops pearls of PPC wisdom in his own unique and refreshing way that feels more like having a conversation with him than reading a book. This isn't a step-by-step optimization guide; this is create your adventure guide to critical thinking about search, the role it plays and has played in your digital marketing mix and challenging you to rethink some of your preconceived notions about PPC. I have been to hundreds of PPC and Digital Marketing conferences and I can honestly say that Kirk is one of a handful of individuals I always listen to because I learn so much from him; I'm as impressed with this book and how he delivers his well thought through views in a witty, genuine, and thought provoking way."*

- Christi Olson, Microsoft, Director of SEM, Global Media

*"The keyword is dead, long live audiences. No, the keyword is alive, audiences are a fad. These and many other arguments over automation, data ownership, and more have been had by PPC managers for years. Kirk does a good job of looking through the changing viewpoints of PPC management and providing many pro and con arguments to what the future holds in PPC. If you are looking for a fun read into the mind of a PPC marketer, you'll enjoy this book."*

- Brad Geddes, Adalysis, Co-Founder; Author of Advanced Google AdWords

*"What I like about this book is that it's sprinkled with personal anecdotes from the life of running a PPC agency. Hearing stories of how clients perceived things we as PPC experts take for granted helps frame the solutions Kirk proposes. It makes for an engaging and educational read."*

- Frederick Vallaeys, Optmyzr, CEO & Cofounder

*"Did you know that the purchase funnel is actually a series of "mazes?" And that there are some sure-fire ways to deal with difficult clients that improve the relationship? Kirk Williams' Ponderings of a PPC Professional is a must-read for anyone who wants to fine-tune their PPC consultancy or agency. The book won't replace your copy of Geddes' or Goodman's introductory masterpieces, but it's a perfect augmentation of both!"*

- David Szetela, President, Paid Search Association; FMB Media, Owner and CEO

*"For those of us working within the paid search industry, it's easy to get myopic. We start to lose the forest for the trees. Kirk's approach to PPC in Ponderings Of A PPC Professional is a refreshing step back from mere tactics — instead he looks at a more holistic view of paid search. Rather than a blind trust of big data, audience personas, and various other catchphrase methodologies, Kirk instead points out the difference between sheer knowledge and actual wisdom. This book is perfect for the paid search marketer who finds themselves caught up in minutia (myself included!) and needs to get back to the fundamentals of good marketing: reaching people with a message, and understanding the technical aspects of accomplishing just that."*

- Gil Gildner, Author or Becoming a Digital Marketer; Owner, Discosloth


*"When I think of PPC marketing, I think of Kirk and his expertise. This book is highly recommended for anyone needing a crash course in why we do PPC, how it works, and how it works in the present day. There are few people with deeper or broader expertise on the topic than Kirk."*

- John Doherty, CEO & Founder, Credo


*"Kirk Williams shares his practical philosophy on PPC in this book. His honesty is refreshing, especially in an industry that can sometimes get stuck in a dogmatic place on certain issues! If you are interested in thoughtful discussion of highly relevant topics, you will thoroughly enjoy this book. Kirk has an approachable style that makes even complex topics easy to understand and follow. His book will certainly prompt some contemplation on how you're approaching PPC – and that is always a good thing!"*

- Julie Friedman Bacchini, President, Neptune Moon LLC


*"Kirk is a treasure in the digital marketing industry and "Ponderings of a PPC Professional" is a one-of-a-kind glimpse into paid search as a whole. Beyond tactics & strategies, this book challenges you to think differently, question (almost) everything and will force you well out of your comfort zone when analyzing your marketing funnels to your attribution models. As much as "Ponderings of a PPC Professional" will help to grow your search campaigns, it will likely provide you more growth internally as an all-around modern marketer."*

- Greg Finn, Cypress North, Partner

"Opinions in PPC can be binary. For automation, against automation. For the funnel, against the funnel. It is rare to find someone in PPC who is willing to stand on both sides of the fence and consider every angle. In Ponderings of a PPC Professional, Kirk does just that. This is a breakthrough book that addresses elements of our industry we do not always consider with relatable humor and actionable advice."

-   Amalia Fowler, Director of Marketing Services, Snaptech Marketing

"If you get into digital marketing thinking you'll win by being data-driven and quantitative, you're in for a rude awakening. Relationships and opinions still matter here, and Kirk understands this better than anyone. His hard-won experience of what it takes to not only manage accounts but to keep clients happy for the long haul will be invaluable to newbies and seasoned pros alike."

-   Amy Hebdon, Founder & CEO, Paid Search Magic

"Ponderings of a PPC Professional by Kirk Williams is the PPC book we need right now. From the very first sentence, I was hooked. Kirk's conversational style combines deep PPC knowledge with skilled story-telling that will keep even the PPC newbie engaged. Covering a wide range of topics from audiences, to measurement, to client management, this book is a must-read for anyone who's ever managed or is thinking about managing paid search campaigns."

-   Melissa Mackey, Search Supervisor, Gyro

"Kirk Williams has written a must-read for those in the PPC industry. Whether you are just getting started or you have been in the game for a decade, Kirk skillfully weaves his philosophical musings with well-thought out practical strategies that you will be able to implement immediately. If you are in the PPC game then you need to read this book (and follow @PPCKirk on Twitter). You won't regret it!"

-   Stein Broeder, Microsoft, Senior Marketing Communications Manager; Author of The Business of Trust

"The majority of PPC content today is buried in the technical side of the industry. Kirk's book is a much needed exploration of how PPC works on a philosophical level. The best PPCers I have been around think more about the evergreen topics covered in this book than the technical side of being a PPC professional."

-   Jon Davis, Co-Founder, Shape.io

*"Kirk is a seminal mind in the world of digital marketing, specifically his efforts around e-commerce and Google Shopping. His classical approach to modern technologies makes them easy to understand, tangible and relatable. This book offers a clever mix of strategic and tactical advice and is sure to become an essential read for beginners, seasoned practitioners and executives looking to turbocharge their marketing efforts."*

- Aaron Levy, Tinuiti, SEM Group Director


*"Kirk has always been one of the best in the PPC industry to share tactical knowledge as well as the many factors in the world that can affect your PPC efforts. This book perfectly ties those two topics together. Whether you are new to the industry or someone who has been working on accounts for years, you will find a refreshing POV about PPC that will help you grow in this profession no matter what industry you are in. Yes this book will help you become better at PPC, but the true value is walking away from this book a better overall marketer."*

- Joe Martinez, Paid Media Pros, Partner

# CONTENTS

# FOREWORD BY AJ WILCOX

I get asked all the time by junior marketers what resources they should consume in order to grow in PPC. One simple Google search will show you thousands of courses by people who lack experience and don't have a reputation to uphold. Now I have a definitive resource to share with them.

Kirk is one of the most well-known and well-respected PPC professionals out there. He speaks on stages all over the world and receives praise (both to his face AND behind his back). He's not one of those business owners who got out of touch but keeps talking like he knows what he's talking about -- no, Kirk is in Google accounts all the live-long day, and also runs an extremely successful agency.

This book is full of gems - there's no BS or unproven theories. He approaches it in a straightforward, and very understandable way. Whether you're brand new to PPC, or a total veteran, you'll get value out of this read.

You won't find an "ode to Google" here - Kirk is a realist and tells it like it is. He tells you when PPC isn't the answer, and where it fits into the whole marketing funnel.

This book covers everything from PPC management to even starting your own successful ad agency, and has specific stories and examples that will make the concepts real and applicable. It comes from one of the most trustworthy sources out there, and you'll smile at least once on every page.

If I had to take only one book to a desert island, this would be it. If I could get it on audiobook, and the island had reliable power and wifi - even better.

- AJ Wilcox, B2Linked, September 2020

# INTRODUCTION

*"We didn't go with your agency because you didn't address the major change Google just made in our industry, and we would have expected you to be up on current events."*

His words stung. Sticks and stones may break bones, but I've never found words to be entirely devoid of potential harm themselves.

I stared at the email. He wasn't finished.

*"Oh, and you sent us two PDFs instead of one, it made sharing your proposal with our team trickier."*

His second sentence broke the remaining irritation in my soul and I chortled. Yes, it was a true chortle. Hey, if two PDFs were going to make or break this relationship, he seemed a little high maintenance as it was. We were better moving on to the next line and letting this fish get away.

His first comment continued to sting, however. You see, I had spent significant time digging into his Google Ads (AdWords, at the time) account to give him insights into how my agency, ZATO, was going to blow his mind with our awesomeness (my words) if he were to hire us.

But as in the opening scene of Jaws, there a clear and present danger hurtling towards me, even while I cheerfully and ignorantly prepared his Account Analysis (we don't call a sales analysis, an "audit" at ZATO. We call it an Account Analysis because we charge for audits, and I see the two accomplishing very different objectives). I may have even whistled while I worked. His industry was in jobs. He was developing a software for a better job search, and it had some potential and I genuinely thought we would be a good fit.

The looming and ominous problem of which I was ignorant was that Google had the exact same idea as he did, and they announced their new "Google for Jobs" platform the very same day (June 20, 2017) I sent the Analysis with our Proposal to the client.

I kid you not! I sent him the proposal in the morning, and I was reading about the announcement on some Search blog that afternoon. The. Same. Day.

Life comes at you fast sometimes. Being a human in digital marketing is hard.

Google can make a change that shuts down your business overnight. You may be running ads happy as a clam, and suddenly they decide your business industry is concerning for this, that, or the other reason and they disallow ads and shut you down.

Yet, after that terrible sounding introduction, digital marketing and data analysts have more secure jobs than ever before. I wrote this book (or at least compiled and rewrote the chapters based on written previously blog posts) immediately after the outbreak of the COVID-19 pandemic, in which online retail remained strong (or grew) as physical locations continued to struggle.

More and more people are flocking to PPC than ever before, and it continues to be an exciting new world for even us old duffers (okay, maybe I'm not that old).

I love the word, "pondering." It means to think carefully, to mentally chew threw something over time. The writing I do in PPC often results in something I have pondered on, sometimes for years.

I wanted to write a book based on those various ponderings, and in doing so, encourage you to embark on your own pondering experience on these various aspects of PPC.

While there are excellent books about the history of Paid Search, and the inner workings of how remarketing audiences work and should be added into an account, I wanted to write a book about the random, important, philosophical things I think are necessary to know about PPC.

These are the random things that come to my brain, the important things that you might not hear elsewhere, but that will make you a better PPCer because they will get you to think about how PPC works. My goal is to challenge some commonly held beliefs and to support others, but above all… to get you to think.

If, by the time you finish this book, you have not disagreed with at least one thing in the book, then I have failed you. I am not a perfect marketer, I will have gotten some things incorrect (which frankly, makes putting myself out there quite terrifying), and my goal isn't to get you to agree with everything I say.

My goal is to get you to think.

If I accomplish that while you read this book, then I can live with the knowledge that I don't have it all correct myself, because I have helped us think through something just a little more deeply than we would have otherwise. Your attention is a privilege I do not take lightly.

It's a brave new world out there in the Land of PPC, so let's start exploring and see where this adventure takes us both.

- Kirk Williams, @PPCKirk

# CHAPTER 1 - PERSONAL, TIMELY, INTENT

*The Keyword is the True Power of Paid Search*

Timing is everything. As I write this, our world is in the middle of a pandemic. Well, truthfully, not knowing when the pandemic will end (will it end?), we could be closer to the beginning than the middle.

In 2020 up until this point, we have gone from life as a relatively normal entity, to a world-wide virus, hundreds of thousands dead, millions infected, 40 million unemployed in the US alone, one of the greatest single day stock market crashes in history, not to mention the protests after George Floyd's murder in Minneapolis by a police officer, and, oh yeah the independent nation of the CHAZ turned CHOP in Seattle.

What does this have to do with PPC and this book?

Well, in a tense era with people tightening their financial belts as many lose their jobs and businesses close down, search is more important and powerful than ever.

This may seem like a no-brainer to the person reading this chapter in 2020 and beyond, but a few years ago there was talk in the PPC world of the possibility of audience targeting (Social Media) replacing keyword targeting (Search). This chapter is my attempt to demonstrate that (while I can't guarantee Google or Microsoft doing something foolish like eliminating keyword targeting) there will long be a place for the keyword and paid search in our digital lives.

I have been chewing on the concept of keyword vs. audience targeting for roughly six years now. In that time, we have seen audience targeting grow in popularity (as expected) and depth.

"Popularity" is somewhat of an understatement here. I would go so far as to say that a few years ago, some marketers lauded it in messianic-like "thy kingdom come, thy will be done" reverential language; as if paid search were lacking a heartbeat before the life-giving audience targeting had arrived and 1–2–3-cleared it into relevance.

Despite audience targeting's understandable popularity and success, we began to see the revelation of weakness as well. We learned it's not quite the heroic, rescue-the-captives targeting method paid searchers had hoped it would be, and that audience targeting would not replace the keyword in paid search.

Before we get into the throes of keyword philosophy, though, I'd like to acknowledge a crucial point.

**It is not my intention to set up a false dichotomy.**

I believe the keyword is still the most valuable form of targeting for a paid search marketer, but I also believe that audience targeting can play a valuable complementary role in search bidding. The best illustration I've heard on the core weakness of audience targeting was from an older traditional marketer who has probably never bid on a keyword in his life.

"I have two teenage daughters," he revealed, with no small amount of pride.

"They are within 18 months of each other, so in age demographic targeting, they are the same person."

"They are both young women, so in gender demographic targeting, they are the same person."

"They are both my daughters in my care, so in income demographic targeting, they are the same person."

"They are both living in my house, so in geographical targeting, they are the same person."

"They share the same friends, so in social targeting, they are the same person."

"However, in terms of personality, they couldn't be more different. One is artistic and enjoys heels and dresses and makeup." He reflected, "the other loves the outdoors and sports, and spends her time in blue jeans and sneakers."

If an audience-targeting marketer selling spring dresses saw them in her marketing list, she would:

(1) see two older high school girls with the same income in the same geographical area;
(2) assume they are both interested in what she has to sell; and
(3) only make one salc.

*The problem isn't with her targeting, the problem is that not all those forced into an audience persona box will fit.*

In September of 2015, Aaron Levy (a brilliant marketing mind; go follow him online) wrote a fabulously under-shared post revealing these same weaknesses in another way: <u>What You Think You Know About Your Customers' Persona is Wrong</u>.[1] In his article, Aaron first bravely broaches suspicion of audience targeting by describing how it is far from the exact science we all have hoped it to be. He notes a few ways that audience targeting can be erroneous, and even *gasp* uses data to formulate his conclusions.

While it may seem like I have an axe to grind with audience targeting, I believe audience targeting has developed (and become popular with marketers) because there genuinely is value in it (when it's accurate). The insights we can get about personas, which we can then use to power our ads, are quite amazing and powerful.

So, why the heck am I droning on about audience targeting weaknesses?

Well, I'm trying to set you up for something. I'm trying to get us to admit that audience targeting itself has some weaknesses, and isn't the savior of all digital marketing that some make it out to be. Rather, there is a tried-and-true solution that fits well with demographic targeting, but is not replaced by it.
It is a targeting that we paid searchers have used joyfully and successfully for years now.

**It is the keyword.**

Whereas audience targeting chafes under the law of averages (i.e., "at some point, someone in my demographic targeted list has to actually be interested in what I am selling"), keyword targeting shines in individual-revealing user intent.

Keyword targeting does something an audience can never, ever, ever do... it reveals (1) individual, (2) personal, and (3) temporal intent.

Those aren't just three buzzwords I pulled out of the air because I needed to stretch this chapter out further. They are intentional and worth exploring.

# Individual

A keyword is such a powerful targeting method because it is written (or spoken!) by a single person (let's be honest, it's rare to have more than one person huddled around the computer shouting at it outside of a livestream of the Kentuck Derby).

Keywords come from the mind of one individual, and because of that they have frightening, personal potential.

Remember, audience targeting is based off of assumptions. That is, you're taking a group of people who "probably" think the same way in a certain area. But does that mean they cannot have unique tastes, say, one person preferring to buy sneakers with another preferring to buy heels?

Keyword targeting is demographic-blind.

It doesn't care who you are, where you're from, what you did, as long as you love me ... err, I mean, it doesn't care about your demographic, just about what you're individually interested in.

# Personal

The next aspect of keywords powering their targeting awesomeness is that they reveal personal intent.

Whereas the "individual" aspect of keyword targeting narrows our targeting from a group of people to a single person, the "personal" aspect of keyword targeting goes into the very mind of that individual.

Don't you wish there was a way to market to people in which you could truly discern the intentions of their hearts? Wouldn't that be a powerful method of targeting? Well, yes, and that is keyword targeting!

Think about it: a keyword is a form of communication. It is a person typing or telling you what is on their mind. For a split second, in their search, you and they are as connected through communication as Alexander Graham Bell and Thomas Watson on the first phone call. That person is revealing to you what's on her mind, and that's a power that cannot be underestimated.

When a person asks Google: "how does someone earn a black belt," they are telling your client (the *Jumping Judo Janes of Jordan, New Jersey*) they genuinely want to learn more about your services and you can then display an ad that matches their intent.

*Ready for that Black Belt?*
*Anyone Can Take Our Classes.*
*Jumpingjanesjudo.com*

Paid search keywords officiate the wedding of personal intent with advertising in a way that previous marketers could only dream.

We aren't finding random people we think might be interested based upon where they live. We are responding to a person *telling* us they are interested.

## Temporal

The final note of keyword targeting which cannot be underestimated, is the temporal aspect.

Anyone worth their salt in marketing can tell you "timing is everything". With keyword targeting, the timing is inseparable from the intent.

When is this person interested in learning about your Judo classes?

At the time they are searching, which is NOW!

With the keyword (i.e., Search Advertising), you are not blasting your ads into your users lives, interrupting them as they go about their business or family time, and hoping to jumpstart their interest by distracting them from their activities.

You are responding to their query at the very time they are interested in learning more.

Timing. Is. Everything.

Thus, to summarize: a "search" is done when an individual reveals his/her personal intent with communication (keywords/queries) at a specific time.

Because of that, I maintain that keyword targeting trumps audience targeting in paid search. Paid search is an evolving industry, but it is still "search," which requires communication, which requires words (until that time when the emoji takes over the English language).

What about Social media? Social media definitely pulls a level of traffic from search, specifically in product queries. *"Who has used this dishwasher before, any other recommendations?"*

Social ads are exploding in popularity as well, and in large part because they are working. People are purchasing more than they ever have from social ads and marketers are rushing to be there for them.

The flip side of this: a social and paid search comparison is apples-to-oranges. There are different motivations and purposes for using search engines and querying your friends.

Audience targeting works great in a social setting since that social network has phenomenally accurate and specific targeting for individuals, but it is the rare individual curious about the ideal condom to purchase who queries his family and friends on Facebook.

There will always be elements of social and search that are unique and valuable in their own way, and audience targeting for social and keyword targeting for search complement those unique elements of each.

Thus, it is my belief, that as long as we have search, we will still have keywords. Keyword targeting has been, and will be the best way to target (as long as costs remain low enough to be realistic for budgets and the search engines don't kill keyword bidding for an automated solution).

Don't give up; the keyword is not dead. Stay focused, and carry on with your match types!

I want to close this chapter by reaffirming the crucial point I opened with.

It has not been my intention to set up a false dichotomy between the keyword and audience targeting, but rather to respond to what I believe has already been offered as a false dichotomy. I believe the keyword is still the most valuable form of targeting for a paid search marketer, but I also believe that audience demographics can play a valuable complementary role in bidding (for instance, audience lists layered into search campaigns).

Regardless, far from being on its deathbed, the keyword is still the most essential tool in the paid search marketer's toolbox.

# CHAPTER 2 - THE PURCHASE FUNNEL

*And Why It Matters in Paid Search*

Declarations of people dying who aren't actually dead isn't just a phenomena of the Twitter era. In 1897, people apparently didn't pay much attention to detail, or Mark Twain and his cousin, James, must have looked an awful lot like each other. When James passed away, and people mistakenly thought it was actually Samuel Clemens (Mark Twain's real name), he had to wire from London the now famous phrase, "reports of my death have been greatly exaggerated."

People have always had a fascination with death, and they love to kill something off. There's a reason only a couple of people (if that) make it through every horror movie.

Marketing is no different. People love to kill off non-dead things in PPC as well, believe it or not. One of the easiest targets is picked on so often simply because it is so significant: the marketing funnel. But is it actually dead?

Well, in the words of Mark Twain, the reports of the funnel's death have been greatly exaggerated. And then exaggerated again. And again. And…

# Why Kill The Marketing Funnel?

Unless you've been living under a rock (stone/pebble/hard surface... outdated keyword variant joke, sorry) in the digital marketing world, you've likely run across at least one confident declaration in the past 12 months that the traditional marketing funnel concept is dead.

Or dying.

Or maybe maimed.

Or at least, shot in the foot.

The marketing funnel, for those unaware, is a concept created in 1898 to describe the "theoretical customer journey" and assist in targeting the right message to the right person at the right time. If, for instance, someone is just curious about your business you don't want to "ask for their hand in marriage" by pushing them too hard for the sale, but rather "court them" by focusing on answering their questions and moving them to the next stage of the funnel.

The funnel is typically seen as four categories (see below) that move from a broad group of people (cold leads) to a smaller, more targeted, and closer-to-purchase group of people (hot leads).

Those four categories are (also known as AIDA):
  (1) Awareness
  (2) Interest
  (3) Desire
  (4) Action

The logic of AIDA is that people who have a desire for your product are fewer and closer to purchase (from you or a competitor) than people who are just becoming aware of your product. Thus, you need to cast a wider net at the beginning to get in front of people, and then move people further "down the funnel" to get sales.

Easy-peasy, right?

Well, sort of.

It had been somewhat widely accepted until we 21st Century chronological snobbists began to scoff it away and proclaim that digital has changed everything inexorably and irrevocably.

But has it?

In this chapter, I want to examine whether the marketing funnel really is outdated and kaput because of the influence of digital. I then hope to prove that in fact, our understanding of the marketing funnel has simply evolved and we see its intricacies more clearly than ever before... while the core philosophy remains the solid foundation holding it all up. I realize there is a lot of philosophy here, but I think that is core to providing a good foundation for our tactical advertising choices... so let's dig into the arguments.

## Legitimate Concerns With The Marketing Funnel

Let's hear from the marketing funnel haters first. But perhaps that's not entirely fair, as there are those who question the validity of the traditional funnel for good reason. The general consensus of the "funnel haters" I've run across is, on second glance, actually quite legitimate. That is, *user engagement with a business is far more complex now than it was in 1898.* This is true, and an important note, though I don't think it undermines the funnel concept. How?

Here is how the anti-funnelist typically makes his case:

*"People can interact with a business in multiple ways on multiple devices (many of those completely untraceable*

*visits), so we need to think of a new way to describe this besides the marketing funnel, because obviously the user journey is more complex than it used to be."*

What I take issue with here is the assumption that the user journey is more complex than it used to be. I would ask in response to the previous charge: "is the user journey truly more complex in the broader customer journey categories themselves, or are we actually more clearly seeing the inner workings of each broad category?" That is, should we rethink the structure itself, or is what we are seeing in its complexity simply a more advanced look into the mechanism of the funnel itself?

I would posit that nothing has changed in these primary principles of the marketing funnel (i.e., the structure itself hasn't actually changed) and it is, in fact, the second option in my statement above.

Think of it this way. You buy a house at 1598 Penn Station that is a complete dump. Your plan is to completely overhaul every square inch of the home and update all of the furniture, siding, windows, doors, and make this a new home in every way. But is it a new home, or is simply an updated structure? In that way, the home is still the same home at 1598 Penn Station. You have just updated the existing structure and even caused it to live up to its full potential. But it's still the same house.

In this way, I argue next that the AIDA structure is solid, even if the drapes need to be updated. So what is the structure of AIDA that remains unchanging as we consider PPC marketing in 2020 and beyond?

Here are the two core, unchanging principles I see in the marketing funnel:

(1) There are stages of customer intent that change over time moving from less to more intentional in purchase behavior.

(2)  These stages of customer purchase intent correlate with the number of people in those stages (i.e., more people in awareness, fewer closer to purchase action).

In this way, I think the best way of illustrating marketing today is an adaptation of a presentation I saw at HeroConf 2019 by my brilliant friend Aaron Levy of Tinuiti (the agency formerly known as EliteSEM). Levy described the concept as a "maze", with the helpful inclusion of the "Top/Middle/Bottom" qualitative intent language to describe some sort of inter-categorical movement (of which is, if you remember, the first of my core unchanging principles of the marketing funnel).

Like Levy, I had independently come to the idea of a maze, and I presented on this idea in August 2018 during a #UtahDMC session. In it, I noted the difficulty in accurate attribution, even in our digital age of tracking. Based on all of this, I think the following award-winning, hand-sketched graphic is the best attempt I can make at expanding on and visualizing the marketing customer journey today and beyond:

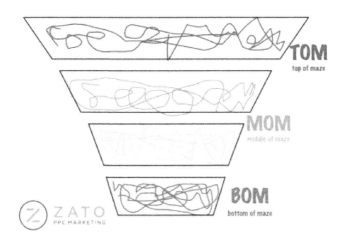

In other words, while there is much mess happening within the AIDA funnel, there is still the overall actual structure that continues... Top to Middle to Bottom of funnel traffic.

But isn't the world of Digital Marketing so much more complex than AIDA?

Sure, we have social which is new from 1898, and email, and paid search, and organic, and in-store visits, and Amazon store visits and all the rest of the things that come with marketing today. But overall, it is my belief that these visits all still arguably follow those two core principles of the marketing funnel.

Okay, so what about PPC (checks the cover again, yup, still a book on PPC and not simply a philosophy of marketing)?

This chapter is *exceptionally* relevant to PPC. It might be the most undervalued chapter in this book. At ZATO, we constantly think in terms of the funnel as we consider what Search Terms or Audiences to target, and what content to show them based on where they are in the Funnel. It informs our bidding decisions (we're going to bid more aggressively for people closer to purchase), and it informs our campaign structure (we try to keep audiences or keywords grouped according to where they are in the funnel for bidding and targeting and budgeting purposes).

With PPC, you can still identify unique audiences and where they are in the funnel, and then craft a message that meets them within that funnel.

## In Conclusion

If you don't see any correlation to the marketing funnel in your marketing, perhaps the weakness isn't in the funnel itself, but in your business audience identification capabilities. Improve your ability to better target your ads to your audience, by segmenting your targeting by the four broader AIDA funnel categories and crafting messaging/creative to support your targeting.

As we consider the concept of the marketing funnel, it's tempting for us in the midst of the maze (mess) we marketers try to track every day, to throw our hands up and exclaim "it's all chaos!" However, I have argued that there is still a broadly identifiable purchase intent progression that takes place in the customer journey. That is, and always has been, the AIDA marketing funnel. Rather than kill it, we need to realize the genius of it.

120 years later, it still enhances our ability to understand the different phases of the buying journey. Even if we have more access into the true mess that is each "phase"... and even if those phases sometimes do shift around or get skipped in the messiness of actual consumer purchase behavior, the overall customer funnel structure remains.

Long live AIDA!

WITH AIDA IN MIND, WHAT QUESTIONS/ KW ARE PROSPECTS ASKING AT EACH FUNNEL STAGE? WHAT ANSWERS CAN WE PROVIDE VIA AD COPY + CREATIVE?

# CHAPTER 3 - ADVERTISER DATA RIGHTS

### And Why This is a Core Battlefront for Marketing in this Decade

With Google's September, 2020, decision to strip Search Terms data[2] insights from advertisers (some agencies have reported around 25%-30% or more of data loss), the frustrated outcry has caused some to begin throwing around lawsuit language. Specifically, there seem to be three main reactions to this change:

1. Those who believe that advertisers own the data outright, or at least the data is part of what they are paying for, and thus have every right to all data. These are the most likely to be outraged, as they believe their rights have been stripped away with decisions such as this.

2. Those who believe Google (or the platform) owns the data, and that advertisers are simply playing within the elected program. These are the most likely to ignore the recent hubbub (or even this chapter!) and simply believe that advertisers should roll with the changes.

3. Those somewhere in the middle. They may not have a hard and fast opinion on who does or does not own the

data, but they also believe that advertisers do have certain rights and the platform cannot simply do what it wants without potential legal ramifications or oversight.

## Why Is The Data Ownership Conversation So Important To Marketing?

While I am no expert on data privacy, and you really should <u>not</u> come to me for legal advice (there you go, that's the legal addendum you expected in this book), I did want to at least investigate data rights and ownership and share that with the marketing community. What I have found is likely no surprise, and why I believe this is the most important conversation happening right now, and in the near future with Digital Marketing.

This gets into the privacy conversation. This gets into the data storage conversation. This gets into the automation conversation. This gets into marketing in nearly every way possible at this time. I don't think it's an exaggeration, to say this is *the* conversation that will shape the Digital Marketing industry for decades.

Personally, I'm happy for conversations that move things forward in helping us be ever safer with online data usage and storage. Though I am admittedly alarmed by legislators making decisions impacting our industry who don't know how Facebook makes its money[3]. How can you properly legislate the ad industry if you do not understand the fundamental existence of the ad industry...but, I digress.

What do I believe is the core question that will most impact marketers in the coming decades? I believe it is this: "*What rights do advertisers have to the marketing data we utilize for our decisions?*" It's not a complicated question at first blush, but the more we plumb its depths, the more we identify additional complications. Let's dig into those next.

# Who Owns Your Search Term Data, The One Giving It, The One Storing It, Or The One Paying For It?

This question is one we began to have internally at ZATO, as we disagreed on the answer. And that is what spawned this chapter. Well, of course the one paying for the data owns it! I scoffed. Then a logical disagreement was brought up and I backed off my (firm, at the time) position.

Is the one who creates and stores the data physically the owner of that data? Who can determine exactly what is to be done with that data? Well, it's complicated, and to my knowledge (I haven't read every court decision in the past 10 years on this) that's still being argued in certain courts. Winning Tech[4] writes of the Microsoft SCA case in which the question was whether the (US) feds could access their data by court order if it was physically housed in Ireland. The decision? It flip-flopped. It seems that physical server location is important, but not the only thing to take into consideration...and shockingly, courts disagreed on the outcome. It's complicated.

Isn't the one who pays for the data the owner? That makes sense, right? If you buy a Big Mac, you get to determine whose belly that Big Mac enters. But in terms of data, thus far it doesn't appear that the one paying for the data owns the data (I'm not a lawyer, remember). Certainly the recent fine on Facebook for inflating video views[5] suggests there are certain rights to data that advertisers have (even if only "the right not to be lied to), and also revealed how important the accuracy of data is to business decision-making, but it didn't necessarily communicate that advertisers own that data.

That being said, throw the actual person into the mix as well (hence, CCPA and GDPR), and this stuff just got even more complicated. You remember the person, yeah, she's the one handing off that data to be argued over by Google and advertisers. What sort of ownership rights does she have?

Here is how I personally (not an attorney, personal opinion here) believe the advertiser's relationship is to data. I believe it is more like a lease/landlord situation.

If I lease my office space, I must own the building now, correct? I'm paying for it! As we all know, of course not. I simply pay for certain rights to the space.

I believe this is likely what is happening with a data rights and ownership situation between Google and advertisers. We advertisers probably do not own the data (that's an argument between Google and the person handing over the data and the Supreme Court); we are only paying for the rights to access it...like a lease. We can store the data we get from platforms like Google, and thus have some sort of ownership rights ourselves to it as advertisers. As a sidenote, that's where it gets even messier. Does that mean there are now two sets of owned data based on those duplicates? I don't know. Smarter people are probably arguing over that now for obscene amounts of money. By the way, it appears that this is also what Google believes based on their Advertising Terms and Conditions.[6]

In short: advertisers agree to very little rights with Google. Of course, that doesn't mean this is legally or ethically correct, but it is an important point for Google, since advertisers agree to the Terms and Conditions upon beginning with Google, and those T&C don't really guarantee any sort of data rights.

Curiously, as I did my research for this chapter I randomly discovered Google used to guarantee some sort of Impression-based reporting in an old version of the T&C housed here.[7] While impression data alone is slightly more beneficial than throwing rocks at a charging Montana grizzly bear, it does mean, that at some point in the past, there was an accepted understanding by

Google that users have some form of access rights to some form of
data.

> 7. Reporting and Statistics. Google will provide Advertiser with password-protected access to 24/7 online reporting information so that Advertiser may monitor its campaign. Google will undertake commercially reasonable efforts to deliver impressions in accordance with the estimates set forth in an Insertion Order. Because the estimates are forecasts, however, Google makes no guarantee regarding the levels of impressions for any advertisement. Google will maintain delivery statistics and Advertiser acknowledges that delivery statistics provided by Google are the official and definitive measurements of Google's performance on any delivery obligations provided in the Insertion Order. No other measurements or usage statistics (including those of Advertiser or any third party) shall be accepted by Google or have any effect on this Agreement. An "impression" means each occurrence of a display of an advertisement.

## The Question We Should Be Asking As Ppcers

This is crucial because, even if we are paying for access in a lease
situation, we should be asking an even more important question
than "who owns the data".

PPCers are looking at Google's new decision to remove Search
Terms from their reporting and questioning Google as if advertisers own the data (since they're paying for it). While frustrating,
it's quite possible that Google is shrugging its collective shoulders because it knows we have no rights to that data (see above
discussion). We are simply leasing it from them and they can determine which data points to turn on and off like a spigot (by the
way, I've written elsewhere[8] that I am increasingly alarmed by
decisions like that which demonstrate Google's lack of interest in
what its partners have to say on the matter, thus showing an im-
balance in a relationship that certainly cannot last forever).

All that to be said, I think the drum we advertisers need to
be beating isn't primarily "who owns the data", though certainly
let's get that determined.

*I think the primary drum we need to be beating, with potentially
more legal precedence, is "what data do we advertisers have the RIGHT*

*to access?"*

If we argue data ownership and lose, game over. If we argue "access rights", it's a new ball game.

## Google's Own Language

Here is a curious thing, and one in which a lesser man (certainly not me) might utilize a statement such as "hoisted by its own petard". Google itself claims in its third party policy with advertisers, that there is certain data necessary to show to the one actually paying money to Google for Ads Program usage. In other words, a Paid Search agency like my own, must share certain data with advertisers in order to align itself with Google's Third-Party policies.[9]

### Google third-party policy

This policy applies to all third parties that purchase or manage Google advertising on behalf of their customers.

Accountability is a core principle of Google advertising, and we want to make sure advertisers—whether they work directly with Google or not—understand how Google advertising is performing for them and what to expect from their third-party partners.

Our third-party policy covers three areas:

- Transparency requirements: Information you need to share with your customers
- Prohibited practices: Things you can't do if you want to purchase or manage Google advertising on behalf of your customers
- Account setup requirements: How you need to arrange your customers' Google advertising accounts

### Transparency requirements

For advertisers to fully realize the benefits of advertising on Google, they need to have the right information to make informed decisions. Therefore, we require all of our third-party partners to be transparent with information that effects these decisions. In addition to meeting the requirements outlined below, third parties must make reasonable efforts to provide their customers with other relevant information when requested.

### Google advertising cost and performance

If the applicable advertising terms of service between you and Google require a monthly performance report for customers, you must include data on costs, clicks, and impressions at the Google advertising account level. When sharing Google advertising cost data with customers, report the exact amount charged by Google, exclusive of any fees that you charge.

If you provide other reports on cost or performance beyond the minimum requirement described above, those reports also need to apply specifically to Google advertising products. For example, if you provide your customers with daily cost and performance reporting at the keyword level across all advertising networks, then you're also required to provide reporting on daily cost and performance specifically for Google Ads keywords.

Share your Google advertising cost and performance reports in a way that makes it easy for your customers to access the reports, such as by email or via your website. Alternatively, you can meet this reporting requirement by allowing your customers to sign in to their Google advertising accounts directly to access their cost and performance data. Learn how to share account access.

Of course, Google is masterful at keeping clearly defined language from sneaking into this policy. It's not like they claim "search terms data is significant" for agencies, and then don't show that data themselves. However, what I gather from this is Google's admittance that an advertiser has certain access to data rights because of their payment to the Platform to use the advertising service, and I think *that* is where the upcoming battles will be fought.

In other words, the question isn't "do advertisers paying Google have certain access rights to data"? Because as I have shown above, Google themselves believes there to be some level of access rights. The question is, *"to which data do advertisers have access rights"?*

This is where it gets complicated, and I will have to send you on to Chapter 4. As a peek into the next chapter, certain data points are more important for success to one business than they are to another. It may be that some businesses are impacted more significantly from losing 30% of search terms data than other businesses. That's the nature of business, and in this author's opinion, it is precisely why the best solution is for Platforms to cease the obfuscation of data for the sake of more automated campaign types that may or may not work as well for all advertisers.

A combination of the two would make sense. Increased advances in automation for those who don't care about specific control and data access, plus full access to the data-sets for those advertisers who believe they need it. This will likely take some work and is certainly not the most efficient way to do business for Google, but it is arguably the best way to do business.

At some point, doing business with so many unique entities isn't solely about efficiency that utilizes averages. Automation shines with grouped efficiency and averages...not shared and thus manually managed data. That is also why social audiences are becoming more popular over and above search terms data with Google (grouped averages are easier to automate well), even though the search term and keyword is why Google has always shone brighter than other marketing channels and is what continues to draw new advertisers to the platform (I know because I talk to them, small businesses LOVE the ultra-targeted nature of the keyword...a targeted nature that continues to be lost with additional close variant changes).

The problem for Google is the businesses who don't fit into those averages, but also have a right to certain data since they are also paying for the ad program, especially small businesses. My question is, *isn't that the cost of doing business with people*, especially lots of people?

The small realtor in Billings, MT, paying Google pennies is part of the advertising ecosystem, and has equal data access rights as the billion dollar travel entity. An engineer's brilliant plan for an automated system that would work for the billion dollar travel entity, but result in the failed account of the small realtor isn't actually the right way...even if it's more efficient for some automated program.

Doing business with so many different people is messy and can't always be boxed up neatly into a closed-system, automated process. Sometimes the best thing you can do as a Platform is to understand that profit and efficiency are at risk, but to seek the solution that allows for the most data points to be accessible so all paying customers can utilize your advertising solution.

At least, that is my opinion.

At some point in the very near future, "data access rights" will likely be decided in a high court somewhere, and I guess we'll all watch with fascination and trepidation.

# CHAPTER 4 - DATA AND AUTOMATION

## And When They Don't Get Along

*"The year of automation is here!"*

*"Don't let your team manually do what should be automated."*

*"The one who still manages bids manually in Google Ads is wasting her time."*

These and other like-minded sentiments are being uttered by PPCers who just a couple of short years ago were (rightfully) hesitant about incorporating too much automation into their systems.

What happened?

Call it evolution of the system (machine learning, by definition gets smarter as time passes), evolution of our thinking as Paid Search managers, or most likely a mixture of both... but the world of PPC has certainly merged into the lane of no return on the road to automation.

In my paid search agency, ZATO, we do a bit of work with automated systems in Google Ads, both in moderated, human-controlled fashion as well as in near fully-automated systems such as Google's Smart Shopping Campaigns released late 2018. I have engaged in debates on Smart Shopping data and automation and written many articles on the topic of Smart Shopping (you can view those articles I've written on my website, if you so choose).

I am especially interested in Smart Shopping automation because I believe it is the next wave of "the new Google Ads". That is, Google wants to utilize more automated systems such as audiences or product feeds to allow them to control more of the placement and bidding of ads than the old school method of keyword targeting. In this regard, I think there are crucial aspects to automation that the PPC industry (and in many ways, the broader digital marketing industry) needs to sit up and take notice... before we are too far down the path of obscure data.

Based on this, I want to dig into four crucial and somewhat contradictory elements of automation of which our industry needs to be aware, talk about, research, and determine the best route forward.

## Why Is This A Crucial Conversation Right Now?

It is a crucial conversation to have now because the platforms want to "obfuscate" (literally, this was the word chosen by Google GM Sissie Hsiao[10]) the data because it is in their favor to run everything. The argument goes, obfuscated data will make for better machines. But shouldn't we pump the brakes a bit and consider this?

I am certainly no Luddite, but the speed with which we are launching into fully automated systems in PPC suggests we need to slow down to contemplate a few things.

Of course, we can't go too slowly, and I think the time for contemplation in this regard is now or never. If we don't discuss this and help our industry develop strong, guiding convictions on the various aspects and nature of data and automation, then we are giving the Platforms free rein to do as they please.

In this regard, the advertising platforms (primarily Google and Facebook, in my mind) have already communicated through public statements and private conversations I have had with different platform representatives at various conferences, that their desire is to:

- Control every aspect of the automated process.
- Keep that data hidden to prevent outside influence on the algorithm.

I think this is problematic for a variety of reasons, as I have written elsewhere in my concerns on Smart Shopping Campaigns[11]. My hope is that conversations like this will help automation continue to develop and do great things while maintaining adequate human oversight and process transparency.

The purpose of this chapter is not to reconcile differences (I'm not smart enough, or have enough background in development to do that), but to reveal difficulties (even contradictions), to encourage conversation, and to get the right people thinking who can work actual change in this regard. The conversation is the win for me here, and why I thought it was an important chapter to include in this book. Therefore, if you disagree with something I say next, great! Talk about it; write about it.

Rather than allow the platforms (with the most to gain) to completely shape the automation process and conversation, let's discuss the following elements of automation (and more!) and help move our industry forward.

## Two Sets Of Necessary, But Contradictory Elements Of Automation

### Kirk's First Opinion: The Advertiser Has Certain Rights to Access the Data

The first necessary element of automation I believe is crucial here is that the one paying for the data has some right to access that data. Of course, I thought this was such an important point that I already discussed it in detail in Chapter 3 (if you have not read that yet, please go back and do so now). Now that you have re-read my argument in Chapter 3, please continue to the next point below.

### The Problem With Kirk's First Opinion: Not All Data Is Actionable or Helpful

Here's the problem with the above, and thus why it is seemingly contradictory, and messy...

What data do you have a right to as the one paying for it? All of it everywhere? Or only what is necessary? You want all of the data, everywhere? Then go buy a server farm(s) for the mounds of junk data that you can't do anything with... for the loads of this, that, and the other data points you'll never, ever, ever use.

*Unlike the trumpeted core value of "big data", the one with the most data doesn't actually win anything. It's the one who can use data correctly who will win.*

We saw above that Google calls this necessary data the "right information" for making informed decisions... but that's complex as well. One advertiser thinks Average Position was crucial for making informed decisions, while another thinks it wasn't necessary and doesn't really miss it. Who is right?

Advertiser A may very well have found value and utilized Average Position well for their bidding, and Advertiser B may very well have ignored it for Search Impression Share and the like. They may have both done very successfully and made their accounts money based off of these conflicting views of "necessary data."

So, who is right? Well, in a way, both of them. They each have their own process for utilizing a certain datapoint in building a successful account. The PPCer will say "it depends", to describe situations such as this.

But according to Google in making decisions such as blanketly removing Average Position from access for all advertisers, whatever Google determines is important is the necessary data that all advertisers get in their accounts. Do you see my concern here?

In not discussing this further, we are handing the platforms the ability to not simply automate our campaigns, but to determine what data is actually "necessary" for us to make "informed decisions".

"Just take your label-less medicine and trust us... it will help you. We're pretty sure. Until it doesn't."

### Kirk's Second Opinion: The Algorithm Works Best When It's Given Proper Guidelines

Well, that got complicated. What about the next set of contradictory but factual opinions on automation? Let's start with the opinion that resonates with us advertisers. That is, machine learning still needs humans for ongoing feedback, even after it's created.

Now admittedly, I've heard this concept spoken of positively by platform reps as well. As far as I know, nearly everyone agrees that some sort of human guideline is necessary for automation. Machine learning isn't artificial intelligence (no matter how many people put AI on their websites). It relies on connected paths from past data points to make the best decisions. This also means it needs guidelines to *keep* it pointing in the right direction.

Free rein: "Make us money by spending money" told to a machine will release it on endless audiences looking for the chance to do just that. It might work, but it could burn through a LOT of money and time while doing so.

Guideline: "Make us a 400% Return on Ad Spend, while spending $100 per day" suddenly sets essential guidelines around the machine's intended path. There are definitions for what success looks like, and by measuring past success from certain audiences, the machine can more easily identify potential wins based on that history plus guidelines.

## The Problem With Kirk's Second Opinion: The Algorithm Works Best When It's Not Being Changed Unnecessarily

What could possibly be the problem with the above statement, especially since everyone agrees that some sort of guideline is essential for automation? The problem is back to the definition of what is actually necessary.

The worst thing for an algorithm is to get bad data. The second worst thing is to change it when it doesn't need to be changed. Manual tweaks have killed many an automated process.

A great presentation on this concept was given by Martin Roettgerding at HeroConf London[12] a few years back around ad testing in paid search. In it, he demonstrated how many human ad testers often make decisions too quickly with too small of an amount of data, whereas an automated process is more likely to see results average (and rise) over a longer period of time.

In other words, we humans can make changes unnecessarily, or without enough data, and mess up the algorithm. Platform reps are rightfully concerned about giving an element of control over to humans who don't fully understand the process. It's a difficult friction in which we can both agree that humans are necessary, and yet also agree that humans can mess it all up. Even intelligent, professional, well-intentioned PPCer humans.

# So What Do We Do About All Of This?

Here is where I would like to again make my request to the advertiser community. We need to see the danger with platforms (such as Google and Facebook) in defining the "terms" of what data is necessary and beneficial, as well as obfuscating the process of the algorithms.

Going back to Smart Shopping (since it is often where my head is at these days), I have heard the previous concern (that is, humans will mess up the algorithm by making changes) used by Google in order to prevent exceptionally helpful data like the following:

- Audience reporting (Who your ads are showing to).
- Placement reporting (Where your ads are showing). Brand concerns, anyone, with your ads showing on some horribly racist website?).
- Search term reporting (What searches your audience made in order to show your ads).
- And even channel reporting (Are your ads showing on YouTube or Search?).

If we allow this by going quietly into the night, the platforms will ensure "necessary information" and "essential guidelines to the automation system" are defined solely by how they want to define them. The platforms are in the business of making money, so that will inevitably impact how those definitions are ultimately established, and we would be foolish to expect anything else.

When the platforms stand to benefit from any party in the auction and they are the only ones who have any idea of what is actually happening in the auctions, we shouldn't be naive enough to expect them to do what is best for everyone else. If anything, perhaps it would be better for automation if data remained available and advertisers thus maintained a greater element of control... even if it slows down the machine learning growth curve and introduces the potential for disaster at the hands of the wrong human guides.

Why is that... for the sake of avoiding the inevitability of our machine-overlord futures? No, I think open data within the algorithm process and more control over of that process will:

- Allow for different strategies and tactics by different advertisers for the data, rather than forcing everyone into the same box (remember the Average Position example shared earlier).

- Avoid the inevitable unethical behavior that will result from entirely closed systems where, literally, billions of dollars are at stake. When that much money is at stake, and in an entirely closed system with only insight into it from internal teams (for example, consider how easy it would be for Google to game a system with a data-driven attribution model applied to Smart Shopping campaigns when they control everything including how sales are attributed), it's impossible to imagine a future where someone at some point doesn't use it for evil. It's just too big a temptation for humanity.

Transparency and process can slow progress and efficiency down at times, but it can protect that progress and efficiency at the same time.

So, by all means, find problems with this chapter, discuss it and point out its logical holes, but for goodness' sake, let's shine increased light on the decreasing lack of data being handed to those paying for it in paid search at this time.

# CHAPTER 5 -
# DON'T STRANGLE
# THE FUNNEL

*When Optimizing PPC*
*Campaigns Kills Businesses*

Perhaps you've heard The Byrds croon out these famous lyrics:

> *To everything (turn, turn, turn)*
> *There is a season (turn, turn, turn)*
> *And a time to every purpose, under heaven*
> *A time to be born, a time to die*
> *A time to plant, a time to reap*
> *A time to kill, a time to heal*
> *A time to laugh, a time to weep*

In these words (little known fact: they're actually pulled from the Biblical book of Ecclesiastes), we're reminded that specific actions often have specific purposes... it's just all about timing. As we think about PPC, I can't think of a more important principle for auditing low conversion rates in your account than this.

The reason this principle is important is because there is a strong temptation for a client who has hired an agency (or a boss and a PPC employee) to become overly fixated on repairing the marketing, when in reality the marketing may not be the problem. It takes a deep knowledge of the account and advertising space (as well as a little guts) to push back on this, but pushing back may be the very thing that saves the business.

If you focus on filtering audiences, or some other marketing "button" to push, when that isn't the necessary solution, you will strangle your marketing funnel and the account will suffer a slow, painful death. Let me illustrate what I mean practically before offering a solution.

## A Painful Illustration To Which You Can Probably Relate

Your client is a lawyer in California who wants to offer a solution for people whose insurance companies screwed them over during wildfire season. You are the PPC analyst, and you identify and bid on awesome audiences targeting people who are actively interested in insurance claims, as well as lookalike audiences based on client cases.

You also dig into Search queries and identify high intent terms to target. You aren't a newb at PPC, and you have ultra-targeted Exact match terms in the account, and even some Broad Match Modified to pick up other targeted queries with the budget you have left.

You have checked Search Query reports and can vouch for the targeted queries sending traffic. In fact, you're killing CTR and average positions on those top terms and you have to admit, you're a little proud of the account. I mean, you nailed it.

The campaigns are pushed live for a couple of months, contact forms begin to be filled out and customer info is sent left and right (think George from "Seinfeld", snapping his fingers). You optimize your bids and ads based on this, and everything is just humming. What a great account!

You smile.

Then the client calls. The campaigns aren't working. What can be done? They begin to micromanage your every move. Is this keyword problematic? Why did you use "the" instead of "a" in the ad? Those Facebook ad pictures should have featured a brunette instead of a blonde. They keep asking questions about, you know, the really important details you hadn't yet thought of that will really move the needle </sarcasm>.

You learn through this process that the contact forms aren't converting over to actual cases for the lawyer, and the client is convinced your targeting is the reason. What do you do?

Unfortunately, I have described a classic, sign-up to subscription drop off. MQLs that never become SQLs.

So what do you do when lead quality dips? There are two primary places you can look:

- Audience (the marketing)
- Post-Lead Optimization (the client)

Let's consider each of these as we determine the best way forward.

## Audience Optimization

In the above issue, your client is naturally going to want to focus on audience filtering because, frankly, it's easy for them to do so. It's someone else messing up the work. It's the third party who must have screwed something up, and frankly, there are a lot of third parties who make terrible audience decisions so they're not wrong in looking here.

In this step, the focus is on the type of traffic being sent. Can we improve our ad timing, ad creative, keywords, bids, devices, or a host of other targeting settings?

This can be tricky, of course, because there is nearly always improvement that can be done in marketing. However, while this needs to be investigated (and if you are a good PPCer worth your salt, you are already digging into this), this is certainly not the whole story, and there is a real danger (perhaps you are now thinking of an exact conversation you've had in the past) of becoming so fixated on the marketing aspect that the client-side responsibility is neglected.

## Post-Lead Optimization

This is the second aspect of improving lead quality, and one that resides entirely on the client side. It takes a good deal of work, and requires a good deal of buy-in (and humility) from the client.

In this, the argument is made that the audience is not the primary problem, but rather the client's ability to convert the audience being sent.

Go back to the lawyer illustration from before. In this instance, the client may attack the keywords you have selected by saying something like: "People who type in attorney rather than lawyer have shown us to be a less valuable audience. They have a higher lead to case-close ratio, so please stop bidding on the word 'attorney' and we'll see that CPA lower and be happy."

This makes a lot of sense (and it actually could lead to a lower directly tracked Cost per Lead), but there is a giant, gaping, account murdering, monster-sized hole in this logic. Can you spot it?

# Strangling The Funnel

The giant gaping hole is that the client is asking PPC to do that which it cannot do: *convince the user of the value of their services...* and in doing so, the request to limit the (good) audience to eke out a better conversion rate is actually killing what marketing is supposed to do: fill the funnel.

*Fill. The. Funnel.*

Yes, the funnel needs to be filled with a certain level of quality audience, and we can't just find cheap clicks from bots in Outer Mongolia in order to fill the funnel. But I know that, and you know that. So let's assume for the sake of this logical progression, that we are all good marketers sending a qualified audience to our client. If that is truly the case, then it's now up to the client to sell that solid audience on their value.

I'll say it a different way: marketers send qualified audiences, but it's up to the website (client) to convince that traffic to convert to the macro-conversion (the main action you are trying to get your target audience to take). What I mean is, if we filter our target audience by preventing certain kinds of people from actually completing the form submission (or even seeing our ads), then we can likely increase the Lead to Purchase ratio... *but we also run the risk of not ultimately filling the funnel with potential customers who should have been willing to convert.*

It's a ditch to be avoided on either side of the road. Neither steering into the ditch of an audience too broad to be interested in your client's product, nor overcorrecting into the opposing ditch by failing to recognize and convert cold audiences who may help grow your brand down the road.

Have you noticed that some brands really just explode? They seem to grow faster than they should, they outpace others, and they just have it figured out. How do they do that?

An account will ultimately see exponential growth, not by limiting the customer base by continually trying to filter out people actually interested in the product, but by more successfully identifying how to convert more of those "other" people already showing interest, but not yet bought in.

How do you identify when it's not an audience targeting issue? The big "tell" is when someone expresses interest in a client's product/service, and then a portion of those who have expressed interest even move to submit the macro-conversion, but then aren't ultimately convinced by the site or follow-up process as to why they would get increased value paying for your client's product/service rather than going off to find another option.

That's a huge red flag.

You mean to tell me that someone made it all the way to signing up for your free demo, but then you couldn't convince them to purchase your subscription? Doesn't sound like a targeting issue to me. That's a person who was interested enough to be interested, but not enough to pay because you (or your client) failed to show them your value.

Don't fix the marketing there; fix the product or offer or content or pricing.

## When To Fix Audiences & Change Your Offer

Now, beware of something that happens at this stage in the game, which is the temptation to turn to Conversion Rate Optimization as the solution.

"We are only converting some of the people who sign up for a free demo, so maybe... let's change the Purchase Subscription button to the color green!" Your very expensive, very young business consultant tells you, "Green means go! Yes!"

This is where identifying the right kind of conversion rate optimization is hugely important. Conversion rate optimization, with the intent of shrinking the funnel, is an account killer. If you think the way to solve your lead problems is by limiting a good audience, then you'll never blow up (in a good way).

This is because you're actually shrinking a solid audience, an audience who was interested in what you have to offer enough to sign up for your first step. Now you still need to convince them of the reason they should choose you over your competition. It doesn't mean they should be bumped off the website so your Conversion Rate numbers look better in your monthly report, it means you need to sell to them!

That's not marketing's fault, and it will never be. Marketing is supposed to fill the funnel with great traffic. The website's job is to convince that traffic why you're the right choice.

So, to summarize: are you sending people disinterested in your product because of poorly chosen audiences or keywords? Then fix the marketing problem.

On the other hand, are you sending people who are searching for the right queries, and taking the right micro-actions on your site, but who do not yet want to purchase? Then fix the non-marketing problem. Fix your offer, step up your email strategy, optimize your landing page speed, change your pricing, or even rethink your business model.

I love marketing and think it's amazingly powerful, but the best marketing won't fix a bad product, website, or offer.

# CHAPTER 6 - INVEST IN OTHER CHANNELS

*You MUST Spend Money Outside PPC if You Want to Grow*

When we receive leads for new clients, part of our filtering system is asking how much of their marketing budget is devoted to Paid Search marketing (the only channel we manage at my PPC agency).

OK, so why in the world would a person who has invested his life in the realm of PPC purposefully shy away from taking on clients who spend all their marketing budget in PPC? Wouldn't we want to be the sole keeper of the keys?

When a prospect proudly states "yeah, we actually invest about 95 percent of our entire marketing budget solely into Google Ads", why wouldn't I hear *"job security"* rather than what typically goes through my mind: *"warning, warning, warning"*?

My primary motivation for being alarmed by a client's declaration of dependence upon the marketing channel to which I have devoted my life is five-fold. We will spend this chapter on each of those points. Here is why you should be alarmed when someone's business rests only in PPC.

# 1. Ppc Can't (Really, Technically, Kind Of) Create Demand

For the sake of over-simplification let's assume there are two core sides to advertising:

· **Demand creation**

· **Demand capture**

PPC marketing is stellar at demand capture.

As we discussed in a previous chapter, one of the things I love about paid search (I'm here using PPC and paid search interchangeably, just because I can), is that you nail the what, where, and when of an inquiry down to the individual level. You can get your ad in front of one specific person (amazing!) just by identifying what they are asking Google. You get it right in front of them when they are asking and marketing shines its brightest.

However, that is when they are asking about it. They had some prior knowledge of something in order to spawn a question or elicit a search. We don't inquire about what we don't know. Because of this, you need more than PPC in your repertoire to actually build and grow a business long term. That is, if you want to create demand for your product, you need to get in front of those people who aren't even asking questions about your product yet. This is the magical part of marketing: demand creation!

And this is what paid search struggles to do successfully.

Here's where I hear a chorus of well-informed, intelligent voices complaining about my oversimplification. There are ways in which you can (arguably) use paid search to generate demand, but I would note that this is rare (and not typically a cost-effective way to generate demand), since keywords tend to get more expensive as time goes on.

In other words, you may show ads for your "Massage and Yoga

Parlor" to people inquiring on Google: "what are ways I can decrease stress in my life?" But, is that truly generating demand, or simply positioning your brand to meet the demand already present? (I would argue the second.) Even if you argue this to be demand creation, you can probably take 100 clicks for that keyword and get in front of thousands of your target audience on the GDN, YouTube, or Facebook instead. Thus to my point on cost-effectiveness.

All that to say, if you genuinely want to grow a brand and generate demand (and not simply survive, maybe), you will want to invest in more than PPC, since PPC is primarily geared towards demand capture.

## 2. Ppc Isn't Marketing, Ppc Is A Channel Within Advertising, Within Marketing

I have encountered people over the years who understand paid search advertising, but aren't good at marketing. In other words, they know how to set bids and choose keywords, but they don't know how:

- You actually find people (or create an interest in people!).
- Position a product well to them.
- Convince them (usually over time) to invest in a brand.

As I have tried to communicate in this entire book, paid search is a fantastic advertising channel in which to invest. It does a great job of answering questions people are already asking and offering the solution of your product or service. However, if this is your entire marketing strategy, then eventually it will come to bite you simply because you need some way to create demand in the first place.

That is, you need some way to:

- Continually engage with people (social media).
- Drip great content over time to remind people of your value (email).
- Invest in what you can grow over time without shelling out cash for every dad-gum click (organic).

And those are just digital channels!

If PPC is the only place you have invested time and money, that will eventually come back to bite you. Find a PPC agency who will care about your business success, not just be willing to ride a quick wave spending as much as they can to capture only the low-hanging "demand capture" fruit before heading out the door. Let's really build a brand!

And to build a brand we need more than PPC.

## 3. Ppc Can Change (& Has Changed) At The Drop Of A Hat

This point can't be understated. You could invest years into an advanced structure in Google Ads that works exceptionally well, only to watch Google shut it down by eliminating some functionality on which you were dependent.

A few years back, I was assisting an agency with one of their clients, and we were seeing exceptional success by segmenting our search campaigns out by device. Then Enhanced Campaigns[13] hit and Google removed our ability to segment by device type (they eventually gave device targeting back to advertisers) and this particular client took a beating in their AdWords account.

Sadly, it wasn't only the client who "took a beating", as they also took it out on the agency with stress-filled calls and hand-wringing—all because Google made *one* change.

*It. Can. Happen. To. You.*

For the love of all that is good, don't put all your eggs into one basket, diversify your marketing and survive the fickle nature of channel changes!

I'm going to speak to agencies directly in these next two points. The previous points can be helpful for in-house managers, or executives to consider as well as agencies. These next points fit directly into the unique agency/client relationship.

## 4. For Agencies: The Stakes Become Outrageously High For Every Test, Experiment, Bid Adjustment Or Disapproved Ad

I invest myself emotionally in each of our clients. I *feel* wins and losses in our client accounts, and I believe my team does as well. However, I have found that, for clients who primarily invest all of their budget into PPC, the emotional toll of high stakes is just not worth it as an agency.

When a client's entire marketing plan is PPC (a role it was never meant to have), it allows for a variety of profit-killing behaviors to occur such as:

- Obsessive, micro-management, communication regarding intricacies in the account. *"I noticed bounce rate on this keyword is 5 percent higher. Why do you think that is?"*
- "Can we have a call?" over every minor dip or bump that happens in an account. *"Should we pause this ad you pushed live yesterday?? Did that cause this morning's dip?!"*
- An increased willingness to fire the PPC agency with the belief that a change will fix things, or something, hopefully, doggone it something, please work, ANYONE...

I have found this sad truth to be the case: the stakes for your agency and personal emotional well-being are infinitely higher when a client isn't diversified in marketing. And I don't mean that in an applaudable, "you got this, buddy, go get em. Reach for the stars!" encouraging way, as if you just need to toughen it up and meet the challenge. I mean it like, "the stakes are so high because they don't understand marketing and are putting unnecessary pressure on you because their business literally rests on your shoulders."

I personally don't want to be in that position because of the previous three points. It's not my responsibility, and it can't be because it's asking PPC to do something it cannot do. Unless something significant changes in that business, it won't last much longer anyway (or at least, your relationship with them won't last past the next big Google change #realtalk).

## 5. A Client Who Cares Solely About One Channel Is Probably Difficult To Work With Because They Do Not Understand How Marketing Truly Works And What Is Required To Actually Build A Brand

Lastly, we come to a difficult, blunt point that I hope isn't taken as harsh as it may sound at first blush. We are all learning and growing in our understanding of how this all works. There may be a legitimate time early on in a company's life, when someone admits "here's the position my business is in with marketing, I don't want it to remain like this, but we need to emphasize PPC right now. Please help us diversify and here is how we are intentionally invested in doing that."

Sometimes startups have a lot of PPC investment to begin because they're trying to rapidly ramp up while they work hard on building out their other channels. That's a great way to start a business, and demonstrates someone understands marketing because they are using one channel to build the others.

Of course, when it comes to startups, recognize that they have their own challenges in PPC, so make sure to walk in with eyes wide open and extra budget for additional communication. Some startups want you to act as their CMO, not their PPC agency, so be especially cautious of scope creep in your agreement where you end up doing more work than you originally agreed to do.

On the whole, however, I have found that established businesses with a significant amount of their budget invested in PPC, have purposefully built a business that way. They've leaned too far into PPC, and it will come back to bite them eventually.

For example, I have observed a certain type of company culture that simply does not understand the first few points I brought up above. Those executives don't want to hear what you have to say regarding Top of Funnel, demand generation, brand positioning, etc... they just "want PPC results!" *"Yeah we get it, whatever, that's not your concern... but seriously can you 3x our revenue and hit ROAS goals next week?"*

If that's the case, my unsolicited advice is to pass on those clients (we'll discuss later how to better identify and avoid bad clients). They will work for a while, but the first issue that occurs in the account will have them shopping around again for another PPC agency who they're hoping "will be the one."

They don't understand marketing, and thus there is a core problem within their business that you, the PPC agency, aren't going to fix even if you hit their ROAS goals. You've wasted significant time onboarding, communicating, and setting up a client who isn't a long-term, viable option. You may find it worth your time to refer them elsewhere right from the beginning.

So, did you ever think you would hear a PPC agency concerned about working with someone who has 90 percent of their marketing budget in PPC? You have now! I hope you take those five points to heart. May they help you be more cautious the next time you meet someone who has invested their entire marketing program into PPC.

# CHAPTER 7 - BIDDING RULES RULE

*Understanding PPC Bidding
Rules and Automation*

While writing this chapter, I saw an article that caught my eye. I count myself as an amateur car enthusiast. If there was a level below amateur, I would fall into that. I enjoy vehicles, and love driving fun cars, but I don't know much about them and couldn't fix the "punkity punk" knocking noise coming from the engine if the lives of my offspring depended on it. Regardless, I saw something about the Tesla Model Y, and I uncharacteristically stopped what I was doing to run a Google search so I could learn more about the Model Y.

While I am by no means a Tesla fanatic, I respect the impressive design and power of the vehicles and like to keep an eye on the prices, hoping against hope that perhaps some day I will own one to tool around town in. As I walked through the process of customizing my Model Y (meaning, I selected every cool feature possible, regardless of the upcharge), I came to a step labeled Autopilot. For a mere $8,000, I could add in the possibility of being driven around my neighborhood by my vehicle.

Perhaps that would allow me to finish writing future books? Or perhaps work on my guitar lessons as my car drives me 15 minutes to my lunch appointment (Billings is not that large, so 15 minutes is about as long as I need)? Regardless, it was a stunning reminder how close we are to a world in which machines carry much weight and authority in key decision making!

If you haven't figured it out already, we live in an automated, machine learning world. If you haven't, it's time to embrace that, celebrate it, and figure out how to do PPC the best we can in this brave new world.

I'm all for better PPC automation! However, this chapter isn't about machine learning (ML). If you want to learn more about PPC and automation, I would encourage you to read my friend, Fred Vallaeys' book, <u>Digital Marketing in an AI World: Future-proofing Your PPC Agency</u>.[14] As good as ML is, it still has weaknesses, particularly when it comes to data quality. This chapter is about understanding and creating bidding rules. What's the best way to destroy your Google or Bing Ads account? Feed a machine bad data, sic it on the account bids, and walk away.

To be fair, that's not the machine's fault. It needs good data to make the right decisions... one key difference being machine learning doesn't (yet) have the intelligence to make illogical or irrational decisions based on the data. It just uses whatever is plugged into it, darn the consequences. The reason this is relevant to this chapter is because many of us do not have the luxury of all managing accounts with great data, or enough data, or the money to invest in a great machine learning platform (for whatever we're trying to do).

In other words, there are still those of us who need to bid well based on manual parameters, AND even for those utilizing automated bidding, it behooves us to understand how bidding rules work behind the scenes. The machines aren't magic; they're just utilizing basic algorithms. We're next going to investigate bidding practices, and then look at two ways to create your own bidding rules within the Google Ads or Microsoft Ads User Interfaces.

# Bidding Basics

Before digging into unique bidding rules, let's look at two basic truths of PPC bidding.

**Truth #1:** **You only have two objectives when making a bidding decision.**

This is perhaps oversimplified, but I think it's worth pointing out to prevent us from getting too lost in data paralysis. The two objectives are:

- **Objective 1:** Decrease bids on low performing entities (keywords/product groups/etc.).
- **Objective 2:** Increase bids on high performing entities.

Admittedly, there are complexities that work into each of those.

- How much should we adjust bids?
- How do we determine what is a low performing entity?
- Are we tracking LTV or just utilizing the immediate data to which we have access?

These are important questions, but really at the core of what we're trying to do is one of two things: (*1*) *Should we adjust bids on these terms and, if so, (2) should we adjust them higher or lower?* Don't get so caught up in everything else that you are paralyzed from making a decision here. Creating bidding rules, even complex ones, can be simplified into these two objectives.

**Truth #2.** **You need to focus on the right data to make a bidding decision.**

We get it by now. We need data. But the person with the most data doesn't win. Data collection just isn't as big a problem as it was previously.

"I'm a data-driven marketer!" Congratulations, you and all the rest of us. Nobody is handing out awards to the person with the largest server warehouse for their internal data. It isn't primarily about data *quantity* (though we do need enough data to make a good decision). It's about data *quality*.

We need to identify which data points to focus on in order to make a good bidding decision. Here's where I think many of us (especially newb) PPCers can stumble over our data. We have access to a lot of data in our Google Ads and Microsoft Ads accounts, and it can be overwhelming as to what we should focus on for simple decisions.

In fact, I challenge you to add every possible keyword column into Google Ads... I did back when I originally wrote this and I got 99 (it's highly likely there are more than that by the time you read this). *99 columns!* If you're analyzing 100 keywords, that's almost 10,000 data points to mine through. Good luck with that.

Here's where the rubber meets the road though with creating smart bidding rules/algos. When I am considering whether to raise or lower my bids (i.e., create a bidding rule, or simply make a decision on a certain audience or metric in my account), I ask myself variations of the following four questions.

## Is There Enough Traffic?

In this question, you are analyzing data points such as impressions, clicks, or spend that ensures you have enough data to make a good decision. If you can't get enough data for this point, then the best way to fix this is to push your lookback window further. Try 30 days instead of 7, 180 instead of 60...etc. Speaking of date ranges for analysis, I like to make decisions based on an immediate look (something like 7 days back), as well as a big-picture look (something like 90 days). In this way, I can identify whether something used to be performing or has always been problematic.

If it was performing before, why not now? What has changed? These are the type of digging questions that separate the newbs from the pros. This question may lead you to something key that changed in inventory of which you weren't even aware... and that's far more important than making a bidding decision. By the way, that's a great illustration of why you are still more valuable than a machine that can only look at the inputs to make a programmed decision!

## Is It Affordable?

This is a tricky one, but I like to keep an eye on general CPCs and average positions when considering bid-setting. This is tough because those are averages, and averages generally suck. However, it can be helpful to create filters for CPCs in, for example, Product Groups in Shopping Ads since higher CPCs don't always guarantee higher profits (often the other way around).

## Is It Profitable?

This is the one of which we're all the most aware. If the Return on Ad Spend (ROAS) stinks, you probably want to lower the bids. If the ROAS is great, you may want to consider raising to be even more competitive and bring more sales (maybe, it's complicated).

Lead gen client? You will likely want to analyze CPA (cost / conversion) based on lead (or even better, based on your CRM if you have one).

E-commerce? Think through a good attribution model, incorporate it into your account, and then consider making bid adjustments based on ROAS (this isn't always the best answer for E-commerce bidding, FYI... specifically in Top of Funnel terms and products!).

### What Is Happening in the Market?

You can't just bid in a vacuum. Your bidding is impacted by, and actually impacts, the other advertisers in the space.

I think including Search Impression Share (and other competitive metrics like Absolute Top Impression Share or Click Share) is helpful for great bidding. The quick and easy explanation of Search Impression Share is that it tells you what percentage of impressions you're actually getting compared to the number of impressions you could be getting.

Why is this important? Well, let's say your Product Group in Ad Group A is killing it with ROAS. You're very profitable and you decide to raise your bids. The problem is, you neglected to look at your traffic share metrics, and if you had, they would have revealed to you that you were already dominating the market, at the top of every SERP as it were. That means you bid up for no reason and could even be over-paying for the auction. Boo! This is key, and I want to continue focusing on it in this chapter.

## Creating Bid Rules With Impression Share In Mind

Here's how we're going to take this chapter and turn it into action in your account. We'll utilize Filters in Google or Microsoft Ads and make our own bidding rules, and also illustrate how to layer on impression share bidding in the mix.

Tip: Save these filters when you're done, and you can easily pull the same "rules" each week or every time you want to run them!

### Bid Rule 1: Decreasing Bids on Low Performing Entities

In this example, we are looking for product groups in Shopping campaigns on which we're overbidding, but aren't converting.

The filters:

- **Cost > $100**: This makes sure we only look at product groups with enough data to take action on.

- **CPC > $4.00:** We have some product groups where CPCs have gotten a little high; let's start there.

- **Conversion value / Cost (ROAS) < 2**: Even though we've sent a bit of money through these products and we're bidding high, they aren't profitable.

- **Search Impression Share > 90%**: Looks like we aren't profitable on these products, but they are showing in almost every eligible search. We've proven that these particular product groups don't do well in their auctions, and we should consider reinvesting that budget elsewhere.

Based on this, we can take this list of highly curated products and lower all bids by 25 percent. Boom! You just found products you're spending too much money on where you have room to drop without impacting other products.

Congratulations, let's move to the next rule example.

## Bid Rule 2: Increasing Bids on High Performing Entities

In this example, we're looking for product groups in Shopping campaigns that we are underbidding on and that are converting well. The filters:

- **Cost > $100**: This again makes sure we only look at product groups with enough data to take action on.

- **Conversions > 3**: This is important because it means we aren't just grabbing products with a random purchase, but these are products with multiple purchases at a great ROAS. Trends are good!

- **Conversion value / Cost (ROAS) > 4**: These product groups are looking great for ROAS!

- **Search Impression Share < 50%**: While we are doing great on these products with conversions, they aren't showing as often as they could be based on impression share. Great news; that means we can push bids up and still have room in the market to grow.

Based on this, we can take this list of highly curated products and raise all bids by 25 percent. Boom! You just found products that are making you money, and yet have room to grow in the market.

Now you are a pro bidder and understand everything about bidding philosophy and market share!

Well, OK, not *everything*.

We're all on this journey of learning together, but hopefully, this has been educational and given you a few good ideas for bidding rules to create in your own accounts. Programming automated bidding rules in a tool is similar to this, especially with varying layers of triggers and percentages of bidding movements. There may still be times when you want to take more manual control of your bidding; if so, this is the best way to do that... even if Google will always tell you Smart Bidding is better.

# CHAPTER 8 - ATTRIBUTION IS TERRIBLE

*But It's Important. It's Complicated*

Ahem. A story to illustrate digital attribution.

Janet likes cows.

Ever since Janet first visited her grandparents' dairy farm in small-town Wisconsin, Janet has had pleasant thoughts of her bovine friends. As she got older, Janet could not visit the farm as much as she would have liked, so she compensated by purchasing cow memorabilia off of the internet. If you could put a cow on it, Janet would buy it.

One day, Janet's friend told her about a new site, Cow Crap, LLC (https://cow-crap-it-all.com). Apparently, Cow Crap would take anything you mailed to them, stamp a cow on it, and send it back. She was delighted, and immediately Bing-ed the term (Janet was not a fan of Google). She found an ad by Cow Crap and clicked on it. 7 hours later, she left the site and headed back to work. She couldn't get her mind off of Cow Crap, however, and she pondered which of her items to send in to be cow-stamped.

The next day, Janet woke up and checked Facebook immediately... upon which she saw an ad for Cow Crap! She couldn't believe her luck and wandered back into the site. Over the course of the next five days, she would visit Cow Crap 12 more times.

*4x through Facebook Ads, 3x by typing the URL directly into her browser, 2x through the emails she was beginning to receive, and 3x through ads in Bing.*

After much deliberation, she ultimately decided to send in her bed frame to be cow-stamped; so she typed in https://cow-crap-it-all.com URL clicked the CTA, and finally gave Cow Crap her money.

❖ ❖ ❖

Now, "attribution" answers the question, which channel gets the credit for this sale? Here is where things get complicated in many Digital Marketing reports, because Google Analytics reports sales with Last Click Non-Direct attribution. When the Cow Crap Data Analysts look at their Google Analytics reports, they see that this sale came by way of Google Ads (at least, the last click was Ads). They have noticed a lot of Google Ads sales coming lately, which makes them feel warm and fuzzy since they are spending so much money on Google Ads.

Their CMO, on the other hand, is fresh out of her previous people management job (Cow Crap felt her "strengths" for this job were her people skills as opposed to her marketing skills), and she has been looking at Channel Reports.

"COW CRAPPERS!" She calls, demanding a meeting. "I have noticed that we spend far far far too much money on Facebook Advertising." When I look at where our sales are coming from, it is clear they are not coming from Facebook Advertising."

"But…" began a low-level analyst.

"No buts," She interrupted. "We need to put the money where it gives the best return. I want you to pull our Facebook Ads and send that budget over to doing all we can to increase our referrals and Google Ads traffic; that is clearly where we make the most money. I want creative ideas on radio advertising, city bus ads, billboards, whatever you need to do to get the word out in a way that will increase referrals. Oh, also, boost our Google Ads budget because that sends sales."

Cow Crap did this, and unfortunately their sales began to dry up. You see, while Google Ads branded keywords sent many sales like this, and thus Google Ads got 100% of the credit for those sales, it was by no means the entry point for most users (think about it, they typed in the brand so clearly they had to be familiar with it already). When they pulled their Facebook Ads budget, they ended up strangling (quite gruesomely, I might add) the Top of their Sales Funnel and drying up their sales. They went out of business, and everyone cried and cried. It was sad.

The moral of this story?

People often do not make a buying decision with one visit, so make sure you understand the journey of your buyers before you make a decision you will regret. Nonsensical stories aside, understanding attribution (note, I didn't say "figuring it out") is an essential part of any digital marketing strategy. Unfortunately, it is also an evolving industry... which means there is still a lot of guesswork and change involved.

When it comes to attribution, I believe there are two ditches that need to be avoided by the marketer driving down the highway. The first ditch is the more obvious one: it is the ditch of attribution ignorance.

## Attribution Ditch #1: Attribution Ignorance

This ditch is the ignorant belief (whether accidental or purposeful) that a user journey is not a complex sum of varying touchpoints with the brand. It often reveals itself as an obsession with last click tracked sales ROAS.

"Did this channel get us more sales, and if so, let's give it more budget."

In our complicated digital sphere, the difficulties of attribution are crucial to be aware of when setting budgets and assigning ROI properly, and it is no longer an excuse to ignore attribution. Whether it be cross-channel or cross-device, we need to get better at identifying how different channels impact our client sales. Going beyond a simplistic last click model in our understanding is essential.

Admittedly, this ditch has increasingly been called out and warned against successfully in the PPC industry. There is still a long way to go, but attribution awareness has been significantly increased from even just a couple of years ago, and I find that even business owners and CEO's are hungry to unpack the puzzle of the attribution enigma in their accounts.

So, to avoid the ditch of ignorance, we veer wildly to the other side of the road... and head directly into the ditch of arrogance.

## Attribution Ditch #2: Attribution Arrogance

Whereas attribution ignorance is undervaluing the knowledge that attribution can bring to your business, attribution arrogance is overvaluing the knowledge that can be gained. It looks at a specific model included in your analytics software of choice, assigns X % of value to each source, and confidently sends a report to the client, "thus hath the mines of mystery been plumbed, and henceforth shalt the budget be setteth."

This is a ditch because it communicates to the client that attribution is simplistic, requiring only some specific, magic formula (which by the way, the one reporting on their channel has clearly figured out that perfect formula, and it coincidentally gives their channel quite a bit of credit) in order for infallible ROI measuring awesomeness to be grasped.

A good marketer uses data. A *great* marketer uses data to take action on what she believes to be true that has not yet been proven (and sometimes, can never be proven), regardless of the attribution model's simplistic assignment of value. A specific attribution model can only take us so far in determining true success of a channel, and therein lies the inherent weakness of attribution.

*The glaring weakness of attribution is none other than our inability to accurately track human emotions.*

By that I mean, attribution will always be limited to the data it collects. when the actual decision made in a sale happens in the mind. Allow me to illustrate this with one of my favorite characters (he was my favorite long before he was made popular by Benedict Cumberbatch!), Sherlock Holmes.

Sherlock Holmes is a master of deducing facts in order to solve a case, but not every fact and not every deduction holds equal value in the resolution of a case. For instance, he may discover fibers on the floor that lead him down a mental path, and then he might interview a witness who lies about a key piece of evidence, and then this might cause him to visit the moor itself, whereby he will put the finishing touches on the case.

Yes, attribution can answer the question: "which factual interactions led Sherlock Holmes to solve the case." But attribution can NEVER properly weight those. I do realize never is a strong word, but I stand by it. For instance, analytics of event facts and user behavior data cannot reveal the fact that it was the witness lying that gave Holmes the *most suspicion*, which led him to pursue the case more intentionally and thus visit the moor, leading to the resolution. Without Holmes (or, Watson for that matter, or really Sir Arthur Conan Doyle) actually telling us what went on in his head, we cannot know his intentions and how they were impacted by each interaction.

The weakness in using this as an example is that we, as readers, can see into the head of Holmes, so we are brought into the decision. This is not the case with online buyers! While you can track user behavior on your site, and you can identify and fire various events to identify who did what, when on your site, you still can never actually know which channel caused the most "credit" for a sale in the mind of the user.

This is absolutely crucial because we analyze attribution data in a percentage model. A Linear model doles out equal percentages of credit to the channels in the entire user journey, and a Last Click model doles out 100% of the credit to the last channel to send traffic, and so on. However, these are giving out credit as percentages based solely on *timing of sessions*, and not on how we as humans actually make decisions... with emotion, with logic, with reason, with desire.

At the very least, one change that needs to happen immediately is fewer boldfaced ROI claims from attribution and more honest communication with clients into the actual state of things. Be less concerned with finding a 100% perfect attribution model, and more concerned with diving deep into a partnership built on trust that will allow you and the client to adapt over time as you continue to experiment and tweak their attribution model based upon source interactions over time and aiming at more directional focused decisions.

So to close, as we think about attribution, I'd like to warn us not to run from the one ditch into the other. Attribution is evolving in digital marketing (woohoo!), but our understanding of it needs to evolve as well. We need to stop simply asking "how were the sources arranged in this transaction?" (that's a great place to start) and instead begin asking immediately after the first question, "what can I learn about my customer's emotional orientation towards my brand in each channel."

Finally, we need to be okay with not having attribution 100% figured out. We can't know it perfectly. We can never know it perfectly. Take a deep breath, repeat that to yourself, and then do the best you can in your client and maybe even, *gasp* rely on your gut sometimes.

# CHAPTER 9 - ATTRIBUTION CONTINUED

## *(Improper) Attribution Can Destroy Your Business*

On November 6, 2019 (immediately before the Ecommerce holiday season), Jesse Frederik and Maurits Martijn took aim at the $129B industry of Digital Advertising, and wrote an article in The Correspondent entitled: <u>The new dot com bubble is here: it's called online advertising.</u>[15]

I remember first seeing the article and glancing over it, but not actually reading it for a week or so, since I was traveling a bit in 2019 for conferences and trying to stay up on client work and life in general. I finally had the chance to read the article in depth in the Minneapolis airport on a layover (when you live in Billings, MT, you only have a direct flight to about five cities), and the skillful writing, and significant assertions captured my attention immediately.

I found myself nodding my head vigorously at much of Frederik and Martijn's article, specifically as it called out the digital advertising community's obsession with chasing tracked profit at the expense of incremental value and actual new customer growth. I'm in hearty agreement with that, and I even found myself hoping this would help push our industry to higher heights in certain areas.

However, importantly, I very much disagreed with the article's premise that online advertising is itself the issue. The authors blamed the failure of marketers and engineers to actually demonstrate incremental value on digital advertising itself, rather than on the tactics devised from an improper understanding of attribution.

> *The real problem in digital marketing right now isn't that digital marketing exists, but it is our belief that we can track everything.*

Here is what I mean, digital advertising is just advertising. It's not the greatest thing to ever happen to marketing, and it's not a bubble.

It's just advertising.

It's doing what marketers have done for years: utilize a specific medium to grow a brand (and thus sales) by getting the right message in front of the right people at the right time. Discovering, as the authors did, that people at eBay running most of their budget into their own (exceptionally powerful) brand terms are surprised to learn they don't see incremental value isn't the nail in the coffin for advertising the article suggests. eBay was just running PPC poorly. Ironically, PPCers in my sphere have long written on the poor eBay PPC program management evident even from the public eye ("used babies" in titles thanks to DKI, anyone?).

This is why it's crucial to point out the thing I believe the article alludes to but doesn't actually identify as the actual bubble: that is an improper understanding of attribution, and how that establishes misguided tactics for paid search accounts that fail to build brands and add incremental value. In other words, I am positing that paid search advertising itself has not failed; it's that an understanding of how to use paid search advertising as part of an integrated marketing mix for individual companies has failed.

Improper use of attribution has led to an obsession with directly tracked results that over time do not build a brand and incremental sales. They simply retarget (not necessarily remarketing, by the way) the same users already in the sales cycle – ad nauseam. In this regard, I would suggest that conversion tracking is as much of a curse as it is a blessing. Conversions, of course, being the specific (tracked) action a user takes to accomplish the goal of the advertiser.

When you can track what source led to a sale, you begin to think you have an understanding of how your consumers purchase, and you begin to invest more money into that source. But what if that source is only one piece of the puzzle... especially if it's closer to the bottom of the buying funnel, meaning much contact has already been likely made by your company?

When you think you can track everything, you begin to shift your time, resources, tools, and reporting to making your trackable KPIs grow, rather than building and implementing the tactics to accomplish an actual marketing strategy within your digital channel. If your paid search strategy focuses solely on sweeping up those bottom of funnel clicks and sales (which is what you're tempted to do with a last-click attribution model that gives 100% of the sale credit to the last source to send you the sale), then yup... you maybe won't see much damage (at least initially) in pausing paid search.

To be clear, certainly, there are times in competitive industries, (especially with startups who don't have more advanced marketing channels built out yet) where using paid ads to initially catch those bottom funnel users is a sound tactic.

I'm going to complicate things even further. You may be reading this and vehemently agreeing with my concerns.

"Death to last-click attribution!" you cry.

However, let me push into this even further. I believe there is no perfect attribution model, and with privacy awareness increasing and dark traffic in a continually strong space, this means you can't really trust a more complex attribution model either.

Wait. Wut.

Why did a person visit on their third visit and decide they "loved this brand and had to have one" because of "just the right" emotional experience? But, then they didn't actually purchase until their seventh visit, 12 days later? Who knows. That's not something you can track. Attribution will always have limitations, which is why in some ways, attribution (improper or proper usage) itself may be the true dot com bubble the authors are sniffing out.

Regardless, as long as we keep chasing solely after tracked individual channel success and building digital marketing strategies (selecting keywords, ad text choices, locations, devices, audiences, demographics, etc.) without thinking beyond individual channel success, then we will continue to struggle to build brands and see incremental growth.

Only when we as paid search marketers strategize with the other channels to build a marketing strategy targeting the right message to people at the right place in the funnel (selecting unique keywords, and channels and campaign types for those, of course) will we begin to get beyond tracked ROAS as our primary KPI and focus more on overall brand growth across all marketing channels.

If what you're hearing scares you because it sounds risky, well then, I think you're picking up what I'm dropping. Real, authentic marketing that builds lasting brands has always been difficult, risky, time-consuming and expensive (with a healthy dose of luck).

I don't think digital advertising is the dot com bubble. I think our belief that we can track everything is the dot com bubble. Time to get back to marketing, and worry less about tracked profit and build a brand.

# CHAPTER 10 – GROWING PPC

*Or, the Tenuous Balancing Act of Profit and Revenue*

*"We want you to 6x our revenue at the same ROAS, by next month. We have lots of opportunity in our space!"*

Have you ever heard this request by a client (or prospective client)? It can be very common, especially in spaces where a smaller startup company sees opportunity to disrupt a major industry. You want to "disrupt" the shaving industry, which impacts nearly every adult in the US? Then you're correct in identifying opportunity; it's simply the expectations that need to be re-analyzed.

The purpose of this chapter is to detail out how I (and incidentally, ZATO, my agency) view PPC spend growth. If you're tempted to blow past this chapter, and yet are simultaneously tempted by the growth belief system voiced at the beginning of this article, I would encourage you to read on, as this is crucial to understand for long-term success.

## The Ascending Seesaw Of Scaling Awesomeness (Or Assa)

The following "ascending seesaw of scaling" metaphor is how I have historically described growth to clients, and I'd like to share it more broadly. To my knowledge, there is no better metaphor or word picture, though I would be delighted if you would share yours with me on LinkedIn or Twitter (I am @PPCKirk, let's connect while we're at it)!

There are Two Key Aspects occurring in PPC account growth, for which an "ascending seesaw" is the best mental image I can conjure.

Those Two Key Aspects are:

1. ROAS and Revenue are conflicting PPC goals in rapid growth (*seesaw*).
2. Your business should grow in top-line revenue over time (*ascension*).

Let's dig into each of these.

## (1) ROAS and Revenue Growth are initially conflicting PPC goals in rapid growth.

First, let's look at the idea of overall PPC goal setting and how that impacts account optimizations. When we ask a client what their goals are in an account, we try to frame it in a way that tells us whether they want to grow their revenue rapidly **or** to focus more on current market share ownership and maintaining profitability.

This is **crucial** to understand as a PPC account manager because it completely changes everything in the account.

*What types of keywords and audiences are you going to target? How aggressively are you going to bid? How are you going to determine what devices, regions, and keywords to pull back bidding on?*

All of those questions and more come directly from this primary question of what your overall business goal is at this time for the PPC account. The reason ROAS and Revenue Growth are initially conflicting goals in an account is because one is focused on saving money, and one is focused on spending it (albeit, wisely). Practically speaking, when we push harder for rapid growth that typically means:

1. bidding higher,
2. finding new keywords and audiences to target,
3. shifting strategies to enter upper funnel auctions (which will tend to have lower tracked ROAS).

All of those have the practical result of surging spend and traffic from previously untapped auctions. Remember, Google and Microsoft Paid Search are auction based systems where you bid for position on every auction.

- When you bid higher, you are often entering new auctions.
- When you target new keywords or audiences (whether upper or lower funnel), you are entering new auctions.

This means you need time + money to make optimizations to return profitability to desired numbers over time.

This is why it's a seesaw.

As ROAS grows, revenue will shift lower.

As revenue grows, ROAS will tend to shift lower.

Back and forth, back and forth... (until your 4-year-old jumps off at the bottom and plummets your 2-year-old to the ground screaming... but I digress).

Let's say you are a company selling high-end $70 razors who has seen a lot of success in bidding on tight, upper funnel keywords such as [luxury razors], [high end razors], [best razor under $100]. You are pretty darn excited about this, but have noticed your traffic is fairly limited. You own the tightly controlled terms but want MORE of the market. You enlist your PPC agency to begin targeting more upper funnel terms such as [best razors] and [razors for men] and [razors for women]. You tell them you want to spend DOUBLE. WOW WE ARE SERIOUS NOW and see what happens.

You're stymied and shocked when you see ROAS drop hard next month, even though you're now spending double. You ask the PPC agency to fix the ROAS, and they tell you they are working hard on optimizing the new keywords, but need more time. You roll your eyes, TYPICAL PPC RESPONSE, and fire your agency. The next five agencies can't meet your expectations either, and you start to tell people that PPC agencies are shady (though in your defense, there are a fair share of shady PPC agencies).

What happened?

Well, getting super practical for illustration purposes, you doubled your ad cost by entering new auctions for these keywords, but in this instance two specific things happened:

- Your new keywords need more time to gather information to actually make the best decisions.
- You entered more upper funnel targeting and need to adjust ROAS expectations to match (Biz 101: you won't make the same profit on a person entering your sales funnel as you do on a person at the end of the funnel, but that's because the person at the end of the funnel also spent more of your money elsewhere making their way through your danged funnel in the first place).

Your additional budget got sapped up on the new keywords, but when they actually got in to investigate, your agency could see they didn't have enough spent on individual keywords yet. This means they just did not yet have enough individual data to make a great decision about whether these terms were actually winning over time (or ad text adjustments, or device adjustments, etc.)!

That's okay and natural, but it's why you see a ROAS (profitability) hit when you surge spend, it's natural because we are locked into the limitations of our auction environment. The nature of rapid growth in PPC is that you have to be willing to spend money to grow your account, and then optimize back to ROAS. However, there is a crucial "ascension" aspect of this that needs to be brought out next.

## (2) Your Business Should Grow in Top-Line Revenue Over Time.

Okay, so rapid revenue growth hits ROAS. Are we just stuck in this epic, plateaued good vs. evil seesaw battle the rest of our business lives?

Absolutely not.

This is where the "ascending" part of my definition of this metaphor comes in. While there is a seesaw shifting back and forth between revenue and ROAS, it should be simultaneously and steadily ascending over time. Think of it more like a ride at the county fair. You remember those, right? We'd entrust our lives (pre-COVID) to rusty deathtraps hauled all over the continental United States with probably little to no safety inspections (I digress, again).

In this fair ride, the "Ascending PPC Seesaw of Scaling", there is a hydraulic lift in the center of the seesaw that slowly lifts the entire seesaw up while it is tilting back and forth (it's actually kind of a boring ride). That is, over time while you are optimizing traffic and revenue to pull back on low performing targets and getting back to your target ROAS, you're also seeing that revenue is a little higher this month. A little higher the next month, and hey look at this, on month three we see our revenue grew and our ROAS is now stable. Wow, it worked... let's keep going!

It might look something like this:

| Month | Ad Cost | Revenue | ROAS |
|---|---|---|---|
| January | $10,000 | $30,000 | 300% |
| February | $15,000 | $30,000 | 200% |
| March | $15,000 | $37,500 | 250% |
| April | $15,000 | $45,000 | 300% |
| May | $20,000 | $40,000 | 200% |
| June | $20,000 | $50,000 | 250% |
| July | $20,000 | $60,000 | 300% |

In the (admittedly overly simplified, I know... please don't tweet me to say this isn't exactly what happened in your account) above model, I want to call out a couple of things.

The first observation being: it is common and expected for the recurring revenue drop to happen along the initial spend increase, but with a measured and controlled spend increase invested wisely, you can minimize the time it takes to get back up to your target ROAS... and it will likely be higher. As long as that matched your goals, of course, you may not care about getting back to your 300% ROAS in the above, and rather want to keep pushing and hitting lower goals. That's fair, but just ensure your expectations match your strategy.

Another important observation you will see between April and May in this example is that revenue actually dips.

"WUT, UNACCEPTABLE, FIX THIS." Someone in the exec team (certainly not you) shouts. Revenue should be going higher and not lower, always and foreeevvvvvvveeeerrrrrrrr. The only scope of reality containing a constantly ascending entity is an exploration rocket shot out of the atmosphere never to return! Everything else in life has natural ebbs and flows, and this is no different. It's good to expect when you surge into new data points (as explained above), that you could actually see decreased REV-

ENUE, as well as ROAS for a period, but here is where it is absolutely necessary to hire a solid PPC team/agency with a trustworthy strategy for growth.

If your keywords, audiences, bidding on their part, and the offer, landing page, sales process on your part are all locked down, then trust the marketing strategy and look to long-term growth. If you literally can't afford to spend more, then don't surge spend. Rather, maintain profitability to save money for a time when you are cash rich and in a better place to take a risk in surging traffic in a market.

Sometimes the best thing (pandemic anyone?) you can do is pull back and maintain profitability while growing savings, rather than think you always need to be pushing. It's worth bringing this out, because from the agency perspective, businesses who try to grow faster than they are actually able to manage with cash are the most egregious for panicking at revenue downturns since they literally can't afford any dip. As we've seen above, revenue dips can (and likely will) often occur in a hard growth stage.

Business is hard.

## The Power Of Historical Data In Ppc

If you're paying attention, you'll notice there is a crucial aspect here that needs to be revealed as we close: the power of data. An account with ten years of history is typically more valuable than an account just starting, and this is because you have ten entire years of data to use for bidding decisions, ad test decisions, new keyword theme ideas, etc.

You can't magically optimize a recently surged spend/traffic account to profitability because you don't have the data for the decision yet and need to spend more to get more data. It's not necessarily because your PPC agency is lazy, or ignorant (though, they could be either or both), but it's because you literally don't have the data yet. Data is immensely valuable, but the only way to acquire data is with time and/or money... and this generally stands in conflict with maintaining a hard profitability number. So I will reference again the point I brought up above which was, ensure that you have the cash to actually weather a rapid growth strategy.

Business is hard.

I hope this has been helpful in considering how to rapidly grow a PPC account. At ZATO, what we're aiming for typically in an account (some accounts, admittedly are in unique places of growth or in a new vertical space and can grow profitability, rapidly as the exception) is a steady ascension over time that shifts between growth and profitability, all the while utilizing the growing data of power to grow top-line revenue over time. This along with other marketing investments such as organic search, social strategies, and the all-important email marketing plan can help establish a brand powerfully over time.

# CHAPTER 11 - CRISIS PPC

*Advertise the Benefits, Not Just Facts, Especially in a Crisis*

After being served my umpteenth "QUARANTINED, ALONE, AND DESTITUTE AMIDST CORONAVIRUS? BUY THIS TO CHANGE YOUR LIFE." marketing pitch on Facebook, I decided I needed to scratch the itch of writing and get my thoughts down. Let's ask the question bluntly that I will seek to answer in this chapter.

Should you discuss a pandemic in your PPC ads?

Expanding the question, should you discuss any crisis in your marketing? There are riots down the street, so do you mention them or not? On one hand you may feel as if you are ignoring society by ignoring what is happening down the street. On the other hand, you may want to avoid taking advantage of a crisis strictly for personal gain. So what do you do?

All of these are questions many advertisers have as they go through some sort of crisis (and you will at some point, if not currently). As I have been considering this, I think the thing we need to do is remain faithful to a core tenet of marketing.

Highlight the ways your product/service benefits your customer, and why they should purchase it. In other words, our marketing shouldn't change based on the crisis, even if our messages shift around. This concept has been around since as long as advertising (seriously, go read the old but good: Scientific Advertising by Claude Hopkins).[16]

That being said, I believe an aggressive run to a crisis in advertising doesn't actually help your long-term brand (and can potentially harm it). As much as you are able, avoid the temptation of marketing to the crisis, and instead lean into the benefits, intelligently highlighting their fit into the current crisis (by not mentioning the crisis).

Let me point to some made-up (but highly relevant) ad examples to illustrate.

*"At Home All Day With Your Kids? Buy our Noise Cancelling Headphones!"*

*"Need Some Quarantine Ideas for Dinner? Try These Three Recipes."*

*"Need a place to store your car while you're stuck in your apartment? Try our Pick-up Storage option. We come to you!"*

At first glance, these ads seem great, right? They are timely, to the point, and get a good product in front of the right audience. So what problem could I possibly have with them? I would point to these four less-than-ideal elements of the majority of COVID-19 era ads I have seen since the crisis began:

> (1) These ads are simply part of the noise, along with everyone else saying the same thing. Literally everyone is writing ads like this, so rather than stand out, you're now *snore* just one of the gang with these call-outs.

> (2) These ads unconsciously remind everyone of the negative experience the user is in, rather than calling them to hope in solving their dilemma. They're using negativity to sell rather than positive benefits.

> (3) These ads may take advantage of tragedy when they explicitly call out the tragedy as the springboard for

selling.

(4) These ads tend to utilize facts, rather than benefits to sell, and thus break the cardinal rule of marketing in never presenting the benefit of your product/service to the customer.

Let's unpack these points below as we all become better marketers.

**(1) These ads are simply part of the noise, along with everyone else saying the same thing. Literally everyone is writing ads like this, so rather than stand out, you're now \*snore\* just one of the gang with these call-outs.**

One of the things we want to do as marketers in order to sell our product or service, is to stand out from the crowd. If you can catch someone's attention, you have won half the battle. You can't close what you haven't opened!

That being said, an ad that says "literally" the same thing everyone else is saying during a crisis, like, "In these difficult times.", "14 Day quarantine", "staying alive in the crisis", etc., etc., etc.... just isn't really standing out at all. You're saying the same thing as everyone else. What should we say instead? Keep reading.

**(2) These ads unconsciously remind everyone of the negative experience the user is in, rather than calling them to hope in solving their dilemma. They're using negativity to sell rather than positive benefits.**

This point may be harder to understand, but stick with me. I would argue that another reason to avoid bringing outright attention to a crisis in your selling (unless you are literally selling something like masks, or something directly related to the crisis. It's okay to advertise what can help others in a crisis!) is that you are subconsciously confirming the negative "hopeless" feelings your customers are battling.

*Your customers KNOW they are in a crisis. They KNOW they are stuck in their homes for weeks on end. They KNOW they are overwhelmed by their children, unemployment, health issues, etc. And they hate it. And you keep reminding them of this.*

Rather than use the bad news to sell, how about giving hope? In this way you will actually STAND OUT (ahem, point 1) from the crowd of naysayers by being a positive ray of sunshine by solving the problems they already have.

Let me illustrate what I mean. Let's say you sell woodworking tools and think this could be a boost to your business while everyone is stuck at home working on their hobbies (those that aren't just trying to deal with small children, that is!).

Here is what the "crowd" is saying by focusing on negativity.

*Ad: Stuck At Home With All Those Projects To Finish? Buy The Best Hammer You Could Ever Wrap 5 Fingers Around.'*

Not bad, but see how it confirms subconsciously in the user's mind how horrible their current situation is? Sad, sad, sad. Let's try again, but this time leaning into positivity and using hope to sell.

*Ad Option B: Your New Woodworking Skill Is Only Missing One Thing: The Greatest Hammer on Earth!*

*Ad Option B2: How's that Woodworking Skill Doing? Make Your Hits Even More Precise With This Titanium Hammer.*

In those examples, we still connected with the user's current experiences without taking advantage of tragedy. It's subtle, but it was there. You don't need to tell them they're stuck at home; they know that, deeply, in the core of their being. Instead, go right to the positive thing they can do while stuck at home. It's slight, but important. This brings us to the next point.

**(3) These ads may take advantage of tragedy when they explicitly call out the tragedy as the springboard for selling.**

Whenever a marketer takes advantage of tragedy in selling, we are simply confirming the oft-repeated notion that "marketers ruin everything." There is a crucial difference between positioning a product or service that is needed in a tragedy (such as online streaming services during quarantine), and piggy backing on a tragedy in our ad text just to turn heads.

Ethical considerations aside, for the points I noted previously, I think there is actually a practical reason not to do this as well since "crisis fatigue" sets in for consumers. In other words, your ads using "coronavirus" in the headlines will begin to be ignored for the very fact that they remind users of all the other ads out there like yours, and they subconsciously associate your brand with a negative emotion tied to that word.

I'm sure we've all seen ad examples of cringeworthy cases. Some car brand jokes about quarantine, or maybe a candy brand jokes about unemployment (not an actual case that I'm aware of, but it wouldn't surprise me). In this case, there is also a very real risk that a brand takes on in discussing the crisis, which I believe outweighs the potential upside.

The question is, can you connect with your customers in a way equally successful to utilizing the tragedy to sell? If so, then the risks of appearing in poor taste or offensive to a wide swath of people severely outweighs the potential upside that can't be gotten another way.

Okay, so what is the "other way" to sell in a tragedy that doesn't risk unnecessary offense? Run to the benefits. Always run to the benefits.

**(4) These ads tend to utilize facts, rather than benefits to sell, and thus break the cardinal rule of marketing in never presenting the benefit of your product/service to the customer.**

If you've been doing advertising for awhile, this is review... but I find myself needing review from time to time as well.

The key to marketing your product or service well isn't simply to post facts about it in front of a group of people. The key is to make the connection between the benefit that your product or service offers to your potential customers.

Let's go back to our hammer and discuss moving from Facts to Features to Benefits.

Hammer Facts:
- Custom Colors
- 350 Year Warranty
- Titanium-Vibranium Material
- Self-Guided Striking

Hammer Features:
- This isn't your grandfather's boring colored hammer
- Longer-Lasting
- Durable, Unbreakable
- More accuracy when you swing it

Hammer Benefits to Your Customers:
- Catch the attention of potential clients as you swing your multicolored hammer, and thus establish a unique brand. Stand out from the boring, normal hammer swinging crowd!
- No more stressing about tools breaking and killing your profit with our 350 Year Warranty. You break it, we buy it.
- The unique 90% lighter, but 150% stronger material we use keeps your arm swinging all day long. Work 3x as fast

and long with our hammer before fatigue sets in.

- Save your thumbs from painful swings and expensive ER visits. With our patent pending, Self-Guided Strike® option, this hammer uses Artificial Intelligence to help you hit your target. Every time!

See how we started with the facts of the matter and moved to the Benefits? In this way, regardless of the time, we need to make sure we are marketing well. That is, identify the way your product or service will actually benefit your customer in this time and bring THAT out.

Don't focus on the crisis (this one or the next). Focus on how your product or service meets the needs of your potential customers (while they're in the midst of this crisis, by the way), and they will naturally feel connected to your offering without feeling like they are being hard-sold. You've won, and you didn't have to put the word COVID in any ads.

# CHAPTER 12
# - STARTING A
# CONSULTANCY

*Going it Alone. How to Start*
*a Solo PPC Consultancy*

While much of this book is open to anyone who is remotely interested in PPC Marketing, I wanted to include a few chapters on starting and working in a consultancy or agency. It's possible you are in-house with no interest in this topic, but I would encourage you to read on anyway. There may be something here you can apply to your current relationship with your PPC agency, or you may someday yourself want to head out on your own!

Being independent is a temptation to many people. Who doesn't want to live life their way, make their own hours, be limited only by their destiny (or, so the voice in our head tries to convince us)? Being independent is like going cliff diving. I've never been cliff diving, so it makes a perfect illustration to which I can relate, of course (I say, sarcastically). But my lack of experience with cliff diving is exactly my point in using it as an example.

The experience and thrill makes us all long to give it a try, but the realistic concern for leaving the safety of firm ground and potentially dashing ourselves on the rocks below entices many to back away from the cliff. Of course, the analogy falls apart here because there are many more variables in leaping out of a solid job and into the unknown in PPC than there are in cliff diving. Perhaps it's more like cliff diving in a dangerous tidal area. Timing & technique is essential in this regard.

Enough about cliff diving. You are likely still reading because this is an area that brings you curiosity. You have considered taking the leap but are trying to determine whether there are rocks at the bottom to meet you, or whether the deep, calm, cool ocean of riches awaits. After all, that's the rub when you're at this point, isn't it? Will you end up like Humpty Dumpty or Scrooge McDuck?

My goal in this chapter is to provide several tips and insights to help you in thinking through the timing and practicality of leaving your secure job and going independent in the wild world of PPC.

### Who Am I To Speak On This?

Well, no one really. Take what I say with a grain of salt since my experiences and circumstances will differ from your own.

I began collecting clients in the Summer of 2011 and then took the 100% independent leap in November 2012. It's been somewhat of a rollercoaster and I've had tons of help from others (including living in my in-laws' basement rent free for a couple of years) so this is my attempt to help you think through some of these things as you weigh these questions yourself.

# 8 Questions To Ask Yourself When Considering Ppc Independence

*"Am I Thinking Realistically About This?"*

*"Why Do I Want To Do This?"*

*"Is Now The Best Time To Take This Leap?"*

*"What Do I Want To Accomplish With This?"*

*"Do I Have Other Business Skills Besides PPC?"*

*"Can I Afford To Do This Right Now?"*

*"How Will This Impact Others In My Life?"*

*"Who Can I Lean On For Referrals And Advice?"*

## **Question #1**: Reality – "Am I Thinking Realistically About This?"

Being independent is awesome. You get to work when you want to work. You work as hard as you want to work. All decisions for the success or failure of your business is on you. If you make a wrong comment in a sales call and lose the prospect, it's nobody's fault but your own.

If you implement a positive change that increases revenue for a client, it is personally rewarding. When you work as a solo consultant and land that big client, nobody else takes a cut. It is all yours. Congratulations! You just gave yourself a 25% raise with a giant new client, and nobody is there to argue with you. It is enriching and rewarding and freeing.

However, being independent as a solo consultant is hard. Really hard. Work never turns off. There is nobody to manage your accounts or answer that email for you. "Sometimes you just need to go on vacation and shut off work." Well, you can't do that when there is no one to manage it in the meantime! Got the sniffles today? Welp, get to work anyway because if you don't finish that report the client is waiting on, it won't get done. I've had to get out of bed before to shut off an account hitting a budget cap. It is tempting to put too little and too much into work/family/everything else.

There is nobody to turn to for brainstorming and second opinions on private data. Nobody catches the mistakes you make, or nobody sees and is impressed by the awesome script edit you made that worked (YAAAAYYY... *looks around empty room, sighs, goes back to work*). You are the minion that must make the change in the account itself when an issue arises, and you are the boss that is responsible for it and has to explain to the client what happened. You are 100% commission-based. There is no "security" of a bigger agency if you lose a sizable client; it just means you lose half your income.

"I'll get employees!" You say, "Then I won't be alone!" Well, sure... then you have to deal with HR type questions and training sessions. Oh, and you still have to build your business to the point of being able to hire an employee (if you are bootstrapping, of which I am a big fan).

I'm not trying to talk you in or out here. I'm trying to make sure you're thinking realistically about what it really entails to be independent. It is rewarding and demanding! Very little in life is free and being independent doesn't mean you won't work. Don't confuse "independent" with "trust fund baby".

### Question #2: Motivation – "Why Do I Want To Do This?"

This is more of an internal question and one I won't spend much time on, but I think it is worth including. A key part of any important decision is motivation. That is no different in this instance.

> *Why do you want to go on your own? Are you hoping to increase your job flexibility? Do you want to work from home? Do you see yourself turning things into a business empire if you could only be at the wheel?*

In thinking through these questions, it would be good to ask yourself whether going independent is the only answer for you, or if a simple job change is the way to go. Are there other job positions that will allow you to do some or all of these things motivating you to seek out independent work?

## Question #3: Timing – "Is Now The Best Time To Take This Leap?"

As in music and comedy, timing is everything in this decision.

This goes hand in hand with many of the other questions I am positing in this chapter. Are you at a place where it makes sense financially? Do you have time now to handle all of the other business aspects as well as keep up with normal account management? Are you currently focused on something like school or a family emergency that will distract you from building a business?

The answer is easier if some outside influence is forcing you into a decision, or you've just been put on notice that you are part of the downsizing effort, etc. No one can answer this question for you, but what is your life like and can you afford to make the change now? If the answer is "no", that doesn't mean it is "never." Use this as a goal to motivate yourself to go independent in six months, or two years, or whenever.

When I was looking into this decision back in 2011, I had multiple things at play and they all pointed in one direction… go independent. I actually didn't want to at first, but frankly, the timing just made sense. Housing, work, school, church, family, life in general all converged in the right place at the right time in a way that worked. It might not be as clear for you, but it is a huge part of the discussion.

What is your current client load? A significant part of the timing conversation is the number of clients you currently have. If you are considering this jump, you have likely done what I did. You picked up a few clients on the side and are now trying to determine if you can swing this full time.

How confident are you that these clients are satisfied and you are in a stable place to make the switch? Or do you have the opportunity to pick up a big client but that would mean you can't do both your current job and all of your clients? That was part of my decision when it was time, I had the chance to take on a large new client and I had to make the decision to remain with my current job and say "no" to that prospect, or take the leap, say "yes" and quit my other job. I chose the latter!

### Question #4: Goals – "What Do I Want To Accomplish With This?"

One last "meta-like" question before getting into more practical questions, but I think it's important in your decision. What are you hoping to accomplish going independent that would facilitate a life-changing decision? If your goal is "to make a lot of money", well, that's probably not a great reason since you can do that working for someone else without all the additional headaches associated with owning your own business.

Motivation and goals are similar, but motivation is internal and what drives you to your goals. Your goal is something for which you aim. I'm not sure if I ever sat down and thought about what I wanted to achieve, but I can say that a big part of my goal system was entrepreneurial as well as freedom focused.

What I mean by that is, I have all of these business ideas and I really wanted to give them a good go. I had a strong desire to create *something*. I wanted to build and maintain a successful business and had what I considered were great ideas, but it is harder to do that when you are working for someone. I had the goal of being the one to decide what to do in an organization. Honestly, maybe that's kind of a dumb goal because at some level we all have to learn to submit to the leadership of others, but it's part of what drove me to step out when I did. I also had the goal of having the freedom to choose my schedule so I could spend time where I wanted, when I wanted.

In thinking through this decision, write down what you are hoping to accomplish by going independent. This may or may not be helpful to you, but it can often help be part of the bigger puzzle of clarity.

### Question #5: Business Experience – "Do I Have Other Business Skills Besides PPC?"

Now for some practical straight talk. Independent PPC is so much more than PPC. It doesn't matter if you can pivot the flim-flam out of your tables; if you can't sell yourself, then you won't last on your own.

How is that detailed knowledge of Google Ads' newest DSA announcement going to get your quarterly tax payment out on time? Someone who excels (dad pun!) at diving deep into spreadsheets, but has trouble keeping calendar appointments may want to consider not making the switch. When you are the Paid Search person in the office, you handle the Paid Search stuff. You probably dabble in a little CRO and maybe some CSE feed management, but that's pretty much it. You do PPC.

Unless you are starting with some serious money (in which case, you probably don't care about this chapter) then when you go independent it's just you. You're it.

*You are:*
- CEO
- CFO
- CTO
- CMO
- PPC account manager
- PPC analyst

- code placement specialist
- CRO expert
- landing page expert
- ad copy specialist
- IT specialist
- accountant
- office furniture shopper
- vision setter
- brand evangelist
- coffee maker
- tax specialist (even if you have one hired like me, you still have to get everything ready)
- sales person
- bill collections
- social media expert
- web designer (unless you have money to pony up for a website)
- content developer
- receptionist
- customer service rep

Clearly just "being really good at PPC" isn't enough to cut it when breaking out on your own. On the other hand, there is a level of learning involved in everything. Who cares if you've never done some of those things; life is an adventure, give it a try!

My objective here isn't to dissuade someone from going independent; it's to warn those jumping in with little or no thought to count the cost before potentially hurting themselves and others around them. If you think there are areas that you need to grow, consider finding a mentor or taking a class specifically in those areas. Set a goal of growing in those areas and saving, and then jumping out on your own after that.

Whatever you do, get better at sales! A final important thing to note in this section is the importance of being a good sales person. I have come to see this as an essential part of PPC independence. If you can't sell, you won't survive. End of discussion! I never thought I would like selling because I'm an introvert. This has become one of the parts of the job I enjoy the most. The more I have done it, the more I have learned that you don't have to be that crazy Type A, ramrod salesperson (that nobody likes anyway) to sell. Just be yourself, be honest, and have fun.

## Question #6: Finances – "Can I Afford to Do This Right Now?"

This is the fastest way to get a quick answer to whether this is the right time for you to go independent. Where are you financially?

Sit down with a pen and paper and count up your expenses. If you really want this badly, cut every non-essential out of your life and count that up. Now count up the client income you have right now. Perhaps if you are about to get a new prospect and this is part of the timing question, count that income up as well. Does your income outweigh your expenses? If not, you may want to reconsider whether this is a good time for you since you won't be able to pay your basic life expenses.

On the other hand, even if you are profitable now, what happens if you lose one client? What is your back-up plan? If you are considering a switch now, the biggest thing I can suggest is to begin saving up. Consider having at least three (six is better, but also kind of a big number) months' worth of expenses saved up in case you lose a big client(s). That way you can focus on selling for that three months, or getting a new job!

The other factor to consider in the financial aspect is the number of things you don't realize you will need to cover once you are out from under the umbrella of an employer. It's a lot like buying your house after you have been renting. "I need to mow the lawn… I guess I have to buy a lawn mower now!" Here are just a few things that will accrue additional expenses that your employer probably currently covers for you:

- office chair
- desk
- computer
- printer
- office supplies (pens, stapler, etc.)
- software (Microsoft Office, bid management, Spotify!)
- a room in your house, or office to rent
- internet access
- better modem, router
- business insurance
- HEALTH INSURANCE (don't forget about this one if in the US, you may be shocked how much your employer actually covers for you)
- dental insurance
- vacation pay
- sick pay (remember, if you don't work for your clients, no one does!)
- retirement matching options
- snacks!!!!
- coffee!!!!!!!!!

The thing to remember when you go independent is that you pay for everything. It doesn't mean you can't do it, but don't walk into it blindfolded! To be perfectly honest, the only way I survived was with family help. There was a point in there a couple of years ago when I was ready to contact some of the agencies I knew and ask for a job. The only thing that kept us afloat was my in-laws providing a place in the basement for us to stay rent free. If we hadn't had that place to lay our heads, I would have been looking for work. The financial aspect of this decision is hugely important.

**Question #7: Personal/Family Circumstances – "How Will This Impact Others In My Life?"**

This involves doing pesky grown-up things like pondering how our decisions will impact those around us.

If you are single, pay cheap rent, and don't really have anyone who will be impacted by a major life change, then the decision is easier. If you have 17 children plus your own parents living with you, then perhaps going with something risky is not the best decision for you at this time with so many people dependent upon your income. I'm not trying to tell you what to do, just trying to use a humorous example to make note of the fact that going independent is a "riskier" venture in many ways for the family person.

It is one thing to lose a client and have to dip into savings as a person with not a whole lot of other responsibilities. It is quite another to ponder losing a client and having your family be in danger of losing your house when your current stable job may provide more security at this time.

**Question #8: Business Connections – "Who Can I Lean On For Referrals And Advice?"**

Finally, the last question I think you should ask yourself when considering the switch is, how much of a network do you have built out? Let me be very clear here. By "network" I do NOT mean, "list of random people you can spam" with emails about your "new adventure" and how they have the opportunity to get on board as if you are selling Plexus or LuLaRoe (shots fired).

I mean, who can you go to for business advice? Who can you go to for sales advice? Who can you go to for PPC campaign advice? I have three suggestions for types of networks I have worked hard on establishing.

(1) *PPC Professionals* – Find people who can be your missing

office mates. Find people who will geek out about search query reports with you. This was #PPCChat for me during my early days, and has expanded from there since then. It is more than just showing up on Tuesdays and talking through an online prepared chat, however. I have tried to get to know many PPCers personally and to learn deeply from them. Because of this, I was able to have conference speaking opportunities open up and many referrals sent over the years. Again, I would warn you to not exploit this community (frankly, they'll often call you out on it if you try). Get into the community, put your time in, get to know them and learn from them. By the way, another segment of this network is opportunities for freelancing. Many agencies offer freelancing opportunities. Get to know them and fill empty client spots with freelancing gigs. This will also help you learn!

(2) *Business Partnerships* – Find people whose businesses go hand in hand with PPC, but who don't do PPC. Try to do this with online people as well as local people. One way I have done this is by volunteering as a board member for certain organizations. Don't just look for immediate ROI from these connections. Invest in long-term relationships. Referrals will eventually come, but more than this, you will be surprised how valuable these relationships are in many other areas as well. You may even make some friends along the way, since life is more than eking business value out of every human relationship!

(3) *Smart People* – This can be living or dead people. Be willing to read!! I have found immense professional value in great books like *How to Win Friends and Influence People, The 7 Habits of Highly Effectual People*, and the Book of Proverbs in the Bible. Reading is the successful entrepreneur's secret weapon.

In terms of people in your daily life, find ones who have a lot of common sense and find out why. Not all of your uncles are crazy. Get to know them and learn how they built their own businesses. The best sales tips I have picked up for selling PPC have been from my Insurance-Selling Father-in-Law. Call up local business owners and offer to take them to lunch to learn how they manage their office or day (don't you dare try to sell to them! This is not a trap, it's you wanting to learn from them).

It's difficult to put into words, but I'll try: When you invest yourself into relationships, referrals come. They really do, and they are usually great quality referrals, but it takes time. Your goal isn't to use people to get a referral, but it is amazing how people are willing to come TO you to ask about your services when you are willing to learn from them and willing to help them in completely unrelated areas.

To close out this chapter, I should probably say something encouraging. If I sound like I'm trying to dissuade you from going independent, I'm not… unless you haven't thought through any of those questions. The funny thing is that a number of those questions are things I screwed up in the beginning myself. I had to learn them the hard way or from the good example of others. So, take heart knowing that it is possible to go independent and survive .

Interested but not quite ready? No problem, save and figure out a strategy to make it happen. Start forming relationships now before you're ready to get on your own. Take on a client or two and see if you like all the other aspects of business life. Make the sacrifices needed to make your dream happen.

# CHAPTER 13 -
# THE ONE ABOUT
# PPC PRICING

*Let's Settle This Debate Once and for All... Or Not Really.*

What would a book on PPC philosophy be without a chapter on pricing PPC services? A pretty boring book, that's what! Getting your pricing right is important. If you mess up your pricing, you either can't sell because you are priced too high, or you can't survive basic business operations and your own mental health because you are priced too low. The problem is that there are a number of ways people look at pricing PPC, but there really is no "normalized" way of doing so, as you may observe in other professions such as accounting.

Let's be clear about something right from the beginning of this chapter: there is no perfect pricing model. I may have to repeat myself on that a few times to make sure it sinks in, because I will argue for a specific model as my preferred model. However, I maintain there to be no perfect model, and in fact, different situations may call for different pricing models. I would expect a 250-person agency to think differently about pricing than a solo consultant, but that doesn't mean there is a right or wrong model that should be applied to every situation. That being said, I believe each of the pricing models contain basic qualities that will make them more or less suitable in pricing for PPC.

To discuss these, I want to focus on the primary PPC pricing models in the market today. Most of these have not changed in years; they are simply the way they are. We will discuss the pros and cons of each model and think through the "most ideal" pricing model. Ready to roll? Let's dive in!

# Hourly

Hourly pricing is common for the solo consultant, in part, because this is how we have been trained to think. We see our value as directly related to our time. This is also a benefit of hourly pricing, because it puts our pricing into the language of many potential clients. We can all wrap our minds around, and make projections for, hourly rates.

Another benefit of hourly for the client is that they know someone is actually working in the account. Someone is "putting the time in" and they bill for actual time worked, not simply a monthly retainer. However, that being said, if someone can avoid working in a monthly retainer setting, can't they also be less than honest on their timesheet? I don't personally buy this hourly rate argument, since people can lie about whatever they want to lie about.

Transparently, I'm just not a fan of hourly rates, as they carry too many problems for the PPCer. With hourly pricing, you will find that you punish yourself for efficiency. Figured out a way to cut your time in half with a spreadsheet on a task? Congrats, but you also just cut your pay in half. The same principle applies to finding new tools to help manage the account. If you decide to begin using tools to help automate a process, then you have just shot yourself in the foot by reducing your pay (and you still have to pay for the tool on top of it).

Of course, some may say that you should find other work to do now that you have been freed up. There is some truth in that, but not the whole truth. After all, even though you were contracted based on time, there is this troublesome thing called "performance" that you will have to deal with eventually. You could work yourself to the bone, maximizing every hour you have, and still end up losing an account if it doesn't send sales. I see this as a classic case of payment/deliverable mismatch. You are being paid for your time, but what the client actually cares about is the quality of your work in the account. If you actually increase the quality of your work, your pay does not increase, and vice versa. I'm not a fan of hourly.

## Project / Task

Another pricing model that fits outside the realm of the monthly retainer models (we'll get into those next), is the project or task-based pricing model. This is also typically seen in consultants, rather than established agencies, though it can be seen as add-ons into an engagement if the scope of work expands. I most often see this model in PPC around account audits. They are short-term engagements with a specific deliverable (the audit); once the audit is completed, the relationship is over.

I am more attracted to the Project or Task based pricing model simply because it has less to do with time and is more about accomplishing a specific objective. If you finish your task in half the time you assumed, you still get paid the full amount. Sounds great!

Overall, there are only two complaints I have about this model, but they are big ones. First, this is the sell-till-you-drop model. If you are a consultant, you have to be selling constantly. Once you finish your project, it's time to find another one, and another, and another. This sort of work can get exhausting and really can only work well within the framework of some sort of relationship with a constant supply of tasks (something like Fiverr.com comes to mind).

Second, like hourly, it does not compensate according to skill. You could do a terrifically horrible job on that audit and still get paid for it. You could identify the one thing to fix in an entire account spending millions and get compensated the same as if you had never found that opportunity, but still finished your project. Because of these two elements, I am not personally a huge fan of project-based pricing.

Let's now move into models that have a recurring aspect to them. I will reveal ahead of time that I am a big fan of recurring sources of revenue. We have had clients for years at ZATO where we get paid monthly, every month. I do not have to constantly sell to replace those clients, so they are valuable to us, just as we have proven our value to them. Recurring revenue is the bees knees, but, believe it or not, there is a lot of argument over the best PPC pricing model that recurs monthly. Let's discuss the different models.

## Monthly: Flat Rate

With good reason, the Flat Rate model is a popular one these days. It allows for an agency to estimate the resources, time, tools, etc. needed to manage a PPC account and give the client a hard number for what it would cost to manage their Google Ads or Microsoft Ads account. It is nice for the client because they can get an idea of exactly what to set aside for their budget projections and keep things sewn up nice and tight.

I really don't have too many negative things to say about this model. In fact, as you will see below, my current model is a combination of this and another model. The one gripe I have with this model is that it is not ideal for managing scope increase, or account success. It still carries with it the same weakness plaguing our previous models, which is lack of potential income growth based on skillful account management. Often in a PPC account (but not always), additional scope will include additional spend investment, but with the Flat Rate model all additional scope growth means renegotiating at the sales table. Call me sensitive, but I hate going back to the sales table with a sale I have already landed. I believe being back at the sales table sends a message to shop around and reconsider options. Hey, if we're renegotiating again with our current agency, let's see what else is out there.

If you do a great job in the account and triple your client's revenue and spend, you get a pat on the back, maybe. If you want to be rewarded for your skillful account management with the Flat Rate model, it means renegotiating, which puts you back at the sales table. I'm not a fan, but we're getting closer.

## Monthly: Performance

The Performance model is a model that attracts many, and maims those it wooed. That's a little unfair, but only a little. Note, this model is making a bit of a recurrence lately, so I spent a bit of time on it in this chapter. I first started freelancing using a performance-based percentage as my model because it seemed to be the elusive, perfect PPC pricing model, since agency and client goals were (so I thought) aligned. The business owner is happy with the growth, I get paid more, so what could go wrong?! I quickly learned there were some gaping holes with this pricing and I ended up ditching it.

Below are my primary issues with profit-based performance for PPC fees. As a quick note, I am talking primarily about profit pricing rather than gross revenue pricing. This is because any client worth their Excel skills will realize profit is key to Ecommerce, not revenue. Revenue means very little if money is not being made at the end of the day, so I am focusing primarily on the profit-based pricing model.

**Difficulty #1**: Who is truly responsible for the sales?

Profit-shared fees assume the primary purpose of PPC is to make sales, whereas the true purpose of PPC is to identify and send people most likely to convert at different stages of the buying funnel. Read that again. Even though it may not seem like much, this is a pretty crucial difference in understanding. The reason this is important is because (most) PPC agencies do not control all aspects of the sales funnel. Sure, we can give CRO advice, and heck, even control a Landing Page. However, that is completely different than helping run all aspects of a business involved in creating a truly desirable product/service priced correctly in a fluctuating market, training a sales staff (who can close sales), and ensuring all aspects of the online presence are primed for sales. When PPC fees are tied directly to the profit, this acts as if the PPC agency controls more than it actually does.

As one (it really happened to me) example, what happens when the dev team pushes an update to the website on a Friday afternoon, preventing people from checking out for an entire weekend. PPC ads are still running and spend is still accruing, but revenue is zero. With a profit-shared model, that would work against the PPC agency for a client issue that had nothing to do with the PPCer.

Another example is in a lead gen company for which we managed ads. We hit and exceeded their goals of sending phone call leads, but they had such call-center issues that they consistently had hang-ups because the phone was not being answered. We were doing our part (sending phone calls), but they were not closing them. Both are crucial to success.

## Difficulty #2: How do you accurately track attribution in this model?

Another weakness for me with this model is that it oversimplifies attribution and incentivizes the agency to make decisions which could negatively impact the top of the user funnel (where tracked sales are less likely to occur). Marketing channels work together in far more complex ways than we ever used to imagine (see the previous chapter on the marketing funnel), and basing pay upon a single channel is shortsighted and irresponsible. There is still a great deal of guesswork and fuzzy math in models for which click should get what percentage of credit. It's especially problematic here, because now we are forcing the fuzzy math to be artificially clarified for the sake of our fee profit calculation.

Practically, the greater concern is that the agency has to fight the temptation to work against the rest of the marketing channels when the agency fee is tied to profit. Bottom of user funnel traffic is a classic use case here, especially, for instance, if the agency would lean into remarketing and brand traffic heavily here.

With remarketing and brand, we PPCers are often only confirming a person's desire to purchase, even though they would have likely purchased through some other channel anyway. In this example, the agency unfairly increased their fees by purposefully investing the client's limited budget in a place that wouldn't truly grow sales incrementally. They only ensured all of those (guaranteed) sales were tracked as PPC in analytics, so their fees could be higher.

**Difficulty #2: How do you get past the data tracking issues?**

Finally, the last reason I am hesitant to use a profit model of PPC pricing is the data component. Data has interesting aspects about it in this regard. Is a CRM, or third party system such as Google Analytics being used? What happens when tracking issues are discovered? We just worked with a client to fix an issue we found in their Google Analytics Shopping Ads data. The GCLID was being dropped, and the Shopping Ads revenue was being underreported by up to 50%. If I had a percentage of profit model with this client, what should happen next? Should I demand the fees for the period before this was discovered and fixed since it was not my issue? This is not a small business, but a smart, recognizable brand. Data issues happen all of the time, and tracking profit and trusting the data (along with the previous attribution issues) is yet another issue here that can complicate things.

Clearly, I'm not a fan of the performance model. The only way I would consider it is how I have heard others describe their usage: they combine two models, such as flat rate and performance, to ensure there is a base pay, as well as an add-on "bonus". I still believe my concerns above would make this difficult and complex, and I find that clients value simplicity (as do I). During the sales process, I want to focus our energy on the value we can bring their account, not wind up in endless conversations about our pricing model. Either way, I avoid this model.

# Monthly: Percentage Of Spend

The most popular pricing model has been (and likely, still is) the Percentage of Spend model. In this model, the agency bases its fees on the amount of advertising spend the agency directly manages. This can be similar to a flat rate fee, in that the agency calculates a certain level of profit they need to make from their fees, and prices their percentage accordingly. Interestingly enough, this harkens back to the Madison Avenue advertising days of traditional media, and some PPCers dislike it because they believe it is an outdated method.

The pros of percentage of spend are many. It is a fairly simplistic model to sell, it is common enough that it does not take a lot of sales effort to explain it (the prospect is often already familiar with the concept), but most importantly, it is scalable. In other words, it allows for the agency to be rewarded for a growing account.

Of course, this is where the most vocal opponents will fix their sights. They will claim that an agency is in charge of managing ad spend, and yet, makes money when that ad spend grows... a clear conflict of interest! This is a legitimate concern, and undoubtedly with untrustworthy agencies, one that has proven itself correct. However, in that regard, any pricing model can be gamed by dishonesty. An hourly worker can lie about his hours. A flat rate agency can charge a fee and never work in the account. A percentage of profit agency can manipulate data or ignore top of funnel users (stunting overall account growth) just to make their results look more impressive than they are. Any model can be gamed, which weakens this accusation.

The response to this concern is fairly simple. It is one in which the agency never raises spend above a client-assigned monthly budget; and if spend rises past the assigned monthly budget, then the client is not responsible to pay the additional fees from the non-permitted spend increase. This is how ZATO manages spend and encourages client trust, and it has worked exceptionally well for us in this regard. If we believe there is a case for increasing the budget, we will bring it in writing to the client and only raise the budget once the client has signed off on the approval request.

Another concern with the percentage of spend model is that

accounts can increase in scale and size without necessarily being a direct result of the advertiser work (for instance, in seasonal times such as the Christmas holidays). There is truth to this concern, but there are also other factors to consider. The percentage of spend model (or any model based on spend) is simply providing a measured way from a third party verifiable entity (such as spend) to assign parameters around a measured spend growth.

In other words, an agency can argue quite well here that this is simply the pricing model we have chosen to utilize, and a prospect is free to accept or reject it. If I don't want to pay extra money for premium gasoline for my car, I can shrug my shoulders and choose to pay for the bottom tier. I don't need to understand the exact details of why low-grade costs one amount and premium costs another. I don't mean to be insensitive here, but, at some level, an agency is its own separate business and doesn't need to apologize for choosing to price a certain way (as long as everything is ethically above board, of course).

The second part of this response, however, is that a spend increase often does come with additional scope (and risk) for an agency! More spend means more data and more optimizations to make more quickly. Do you know why the Christmas holiday season is so crazy for agencies? Because with the spend spikes come increased focus on setting up and running promotions, monitoring and jumping more quickly onto troubled campaigns and accounts, and a host of additional work that comes with November and December. We get paid more as an agency in November, but that is also the month we work the hardest. We see this happen in normal spend growth as well. We have clients where we have doubled spend in a year, and that means we are always doing more work in those accounts than the year before. If you are getting data twice as fast, you need to be making optimizations twice as fast, which means more work. It doesn't always equate to the same amount of work, but that gets back to the things we have discussed previously on pricing according to return, and to skill, as well as to workload. You may have just done a fantastic job and increased profits. Hey, if the client is delighted and you got an extra bonus based on your normal pricing model, then that's a classic case of "everyone wins".

A final thought on this model is that increased spend comes with increased risk as well. Agencies who manage millions carry far more risk than agencies who manage hundreds, and that should undoubtedly be reflected in their pricing models.

## My Ideal Model (Currently)

The model I currently employ in my agency is a combination of a few models, but primarily it is a "Flat Rate Based on Spend" model. We do employ some hourly pricing when it comes to communication, as we find it hard to price communication in other models since it is actually the time put into the communication that is key. Regardless, our primary model is a combination of percentage of spend and flat rate. In other words, I want to have my cake and eat it, too!

I see much value in a model that allows growth in fees without having to consistently hit up our clients for more cash. It is rare, almost unheard of, for ZATO to raise rates on our clients. This is because naturally over time our work in the accounts will help grow the spend, and our rates naturally raise. It's historically been a healthy, symbiotic relationship for us and our clients since a rising tide lifts all ships.

Let me show you specifically how we charge. With our model, we incorporate a Tiered structure similar to the following example:

| Tier Levels | Monthly Ad Spend (paid to Media Channels) | Agency Fee (paid to ZATO®) |
|---|---|---|
| Tier 1 | $0 to $9 | $1 |
| Tier 2 | $10 to $14 | $5 |
| Tier 3 | $15 to $19 | $10 |
| Tier 4 | $20 & Up | Additional $5 fee for each additional $10 in spend |

As you can see in this example (these are not our prices, ha!), we use actual ad spend as a rate of growth to evaluate where the client fees will be. We then charge according to those and account for even the most aggressive spend goals. It is exceptionally rare, but there have been a few times in the history of our agency when spend artificially rose higher than our client budget and lifted them into the next payment Tier. We noted it in our report, and we did not charge them for the additional jump in Tiers. We could have easily hidden it and they would never have known, but when we owned up to it and reported it, the points we won for trust easily outweighed the few extra dollars we would have taken away with our dishonesty.

Overall, we have found that our clients understand and accept this model, especially when they control the spend. It's been one we have settled into after years of searching, and I would encourage you to consider it as well.

Before wrapping up this chapter, it is worth noting two random things to get you thinking.

First, with this model, we always charge a setup fee for the amount of extra work we do in every account we take over. I go into this more in depth in the next chapter on Contracts, so be watching for that.

Second, consider automated credit card payments, especially

if they are prepaid. I have begun experimenting with a software (Moonclerk.com), along with Stripe, to charge automated payments to clients, pre-paying the month ahead. We have about half of our clients moved over to this billing interface (as a bonus tool suggestion, I also use Commerce Sync to import my Stripe payments into Quickbooks automatically for my bookkeeping). Of course, this gets a little complex with our flat rate based on spend model since it is prepaid, but we're working on that! Regardless, being able to spend less time invoicing and chasing down overdue invoices is worth its weight in gold.

Whatever you do, don't settle for a pricing model that limits your ability to be paid what you are worth. Find a model that works for you, and then be willing to keep thinking about making it better. Maybe if we all keep chasing the perfect model, we'll actually find it.

# CHAPTER 14 - THE ONE ABOUT PPC CONTRACTS

*To Contract, or Not to Contract*

As we continue to think through things in PPC Land in terms of general philosophical conversations, especially in the realm of client/agency relationships, I thought it would be helpful to discuss how ZATO keeps clients over long periods of time, when we don't require long-term commitments.

Per usual, I want to be as transparent as I can be so you can understand a little of how ZATO "ticks" in this regard. I'd also like to think through something with you that could be improved in our industry. I'm talking about client contracts. Specifically, do you need a long-term contract in order to keep clients on your agency books?

At ZATO, we have no long-term commitments. Not one. Each one of our clients (biggest to smallest) is on a month-to-month basis with a 30 Day Written Out. You want to walk away from ZATO with all of your accounts and data? Drop us an email with your intentions, pay off any balance, and in 30 Days you leave with no legally binding... anything.

The first question that comes to people's minds (those who don't openly scoff when they hear we don't require long-term commitments) is, "HOW DO YOU KEEP YOUR CLIENTS?" Well first, three important facts to demonstrate this isn't a naive attempt by a startup:

1. Our normal Full Service client tenure with ZATO is measured in years, not months.
2. Our very first client is still with us. They signed on in 2011 and we're approaching nearly a <u>decade</u> with them at time of writing this book.
3. We have multiple clients who have been with us longer than five years.

So how do we keep clients when we don't force them into a long-term contractual relationship?

# 3 Ways To Maintain Relationships Beyond A Contract

We lean into three things that allow us to maintain solid relationships without holding a contract over our clients' heads:

We vet new clients exhaustively.

We price ourselves competitively.

We service our clients fastidiously.

### Client Pre-filtering

While we don't hit a homerun every time, we really do believe in "client/culture fit". We utilize various questions in our process to determine if a client will be a good ZATO fit, and if so, we pursue a relationship with them. This ensures from the beginning that we're more likely to be satisfied with each other.

As one example, while we have grown accounts rapidly before, we're typically not interested in startups who contact us saying they want to triple their revenue in the first six months. That is a recipe for frustration and poorly managed expectations, and we pass on those opportunities rather than take them on and waste all our energy chasing difficult, if not impossible, expectations of growth.

I'm not saying it's objectively wrong for them to have that perspective. I'm saying that's not a good fit with our team, our process, and our own objectives, so we honestly communicate that to them.

## Competitive Pricing

We believe in pricing our services in a way that demonstrates our value, but isn't so aggressively expensive that it is easy for a client to leave us simply because they could save money.

Typically, we've found ZATO to be in the middle of the pack for PPC Agency pricing. That's okay with us, because with the 3rd point, it means we're even more likely to keep clients for a LONG time without a legal document forcing them to stay. This may be an important note for you to consider in this chapter and your own pricing model, as it may change based on how you position your own agency in the market.

## Happy Clients Stay

The final piece of the 3-pronged "no long-term agreement" tactic I propose is that a happy client will rarely leave an agency unless there is some external, unavoidable influence, such as pandemic or change of ownership. Once we actually land a client, we work hard to put all of our expertise into really "destroying" it (in a good way, like how the word "sick" was used to discuss only the most stellar skateboard moves on the pavement) on their account.

While this doesn't mean we put up with unreasonable expectations in terms of over communication or constantly changing goals (we'll have a heart-to-heart conversation if that happens), we do think it means that we do our very best to work hard to exceed our clients' goals. We like to say it like this, "we want our clients to stay with us because they're happy with our work, not because we're holding it over their heads with some legal document."

I think that is really a crucial statement, as your clients typically are not sitting around bored to tears and looking for a chance to have to fire their PPC agency and find, vet, and onboard a new one. It's actually easier for them to keep you as the agency, if you don't give them a reason to look elsewhere (most of the time).

### So, Still Have a Contract, or Nah?

Wait, so should we use a contract at all? Is a contract a pointless document that should be avoided? Great questions! While I am personally against long-term commitments, I stand firmly behind signing a legal contract. This is because I value the power of the written agreement. The purpose of our contracts is not to force an unhappy person to work with us longer than they want (as in the long-term agreement), *it is to clarify the agreement to which we all discussed in the beginning in terms of pricing, objectives, and management process to make sure we all begin on the same page.* This is a crucial difference. The PPC contract (in my potentially naïve opinion) is primarily about defining the relationship and preserving the intent of the relationship, not primarily about forcing an unhappy party to remain in business for an extended period of time.

Admittedly, this has its own risks, and it is why we vet our clients so purposefully. We care about working with clients who won't likely screw us over, just as they desire the same (Do unto others, and all that)!

If you have a lawyer with which you already contract, then talk to her about creating a contract for you. You can also use an online service like RocketLawyer.com to draft a template you can later edit to fit your specific needs. This ensures you get the overall "legalese" elements in the contract, but you can save the template and edit the custom elements such as deliverables or client details.

By the way, this is also why we charge a setup fee for our initial work. If you are contemplating going down the route of no long-term commitments, I would encourage you to consider the same. We want to ensure our initial onboarding value is met, which allows us to have more freedom in offering a short-term commitment. We don't spread out all of our initial onboarding work in pricing over the next 18 months of our arrangement, since we don't require an 18-month contract to be signed. Someone can leave at any time, but it does mean they pay us for that initial setup right away to ensure we are paid for our work, even if someone leaves more quickly than anticipated.

At the end of the day, I believe the best partnerships are built around trust rather than legal agreements. This doesn't mean I don't value the power of a good legal agreement to clarify the arrangement, but it does mean my agency won't be hiding behind a legal agreement if you are unhappy with our management. I value good relationships with our clients, and frankly, I'm not happy if they're not happy. *So why would I string an unhappy client along and keep them, miserable, for another year because they "have to" stick to some long-term contract?* Talk about a recipe for disaster! Everyone is miserable and we're stuck working together for another year.

Call it a "Satisfaction Guarantee" or whatever you want to call it, but we give you the ability to leave our services at any time with a 30-day written email or letter. That's all it takes, but you better believe we'll work pretty darn hard to keep you so happy you won't ever want to get to that place.

# CHAPTER 15 - AVOIDING BAD CLIENTS

*Tough Talk: How to Identify (and Avoid) Bad Clients*

Let's talk about "bad" clients.

These kinds of chapters are always dangerous. I try to avoid them, to be honest, because it's difficult to walk the tightrope of tact and truth. You either end up sounding like a big, irritable jerk, or you fearfully dance around feelings so much that you don't ever really say what you mean. I shall attempt to not fall into either ditch.

The purpose of this chapter is not simply to gather constituents from the various PPC agencies out there who want to moan about poor relationships around drinks in a dimly lit place where everyone knows your name. The purpose is to speak to PPC agencies, as well as to those looking for a new PPC agency, in order to encourage us all to avoid certain methods of communication that will prevent us from having long and fruitful relationships with our clients/agencies.

As I have done my fair share of PPC selling over the past several years, I've come to identify certain statements made by potential clients that make me run for the hills. I'm serious that when I see these traits, I am immediately on guard because I have found that getting rid of a difficult client can be far more costly than potentially losing out on a legitimate client. What are these potentially partnership-killing statements?

## 8 Partnership-Killing Statements To Be Wary Of When Selling Ppc

**Statement #1**: "...just one more question... (after which, 590 questions later)."

Questions are an important part of any beginning partnership as they facilitate better communication. Do we see eye to eye on this? Am I understanding you correctly? These questions (and many more) are absolutely essential when considering a client for PPC... and when considering an agency as a client! But at some point, I begin to be wary when someone won't stop asking questions.

You know the type. They are afraid to commit and are praying you blow their mind or reveal your idiocy with each new question. They just want to be convinced they are making the right decision! Getting beyond poking a little fun at this personality type, the problem here is that it reveals indecision and an inability in the prospect to take basic levels of information (there are *always* important questions/discussion that happen in any sales process) and use that to make an informed decision, and then own the decision.

Unfortunately, landing this type of client doesn't make the questions go away... it will instead further emphasize the indecision and anxiety felt on the client's part. You may find your billable time (and the time of your client) begun to be spent more in explaining random account intricacies, than in actual account management. That is bad news for both parties! *Beware of the prospect who fears committal, which can come through in an exhausting number of pre-sale questions.*

## Statement #2: "I don't have specific goals in mind; I just want to see how things go first."

This may seem innocent at first, but it is often an omen of disaster.

Sure, if you knock it out of the park because competition is low and there is high demand and great profit, then everyone is happy (well, maybe not even then). The problem is when reality kicks in and it turns into a, you know, normal account. This provides prime real estate for bitterness and irritation to seep into the relationship since the client is "not happy", but they have given you no direction as to how to make them happy.

If we move past the initial concerns shared above, the bigger picture here is that you are thinking about partnering with a client who does business in a way that promotes mushy numbers and feelings of happiness as success. Note that I'm not riffing on people who like being happy. I'm riffing on people who have such an unclear understanding of their own business goals that they are potentially ignorant ("I don't know how to think this through") or lazy ("I don't want to think this through"). Both of those speak at a deeper level as to why this should be a warning statement when you are talking to a prospect. Trouble ahead! *Beware of the prospect who doesn't know what success on your part will look like.*

## Statement #3: "We have no history of goals, but here is the exact ROI you will have to hit in two months."

This is the flip side of the previous statement. Whereas the previous prospect was noncommittal, this one moves forward with confidence, asserting exactly what needs to happen in the account… whether realistic or not.

Admittedly, this one is a bit subjective, so take my thoughts with a grain of salt. I'm not concerned by someone who wants their advertising account to be profitable, since, you know, that's what we're trying to do here. What I'm talking about is the prospect who is going to be unwilling to learn of the intricacies of search and gathering data/spend over time (especially in new accounts) and has an arbitrary and unrealistic timeline in his mind.

The core problem here is that this is revealing a lack of general understanding in this new client that marketing is complicated and risky. There are many new accounts that behave differently than the way the Keyword Planner projects the CPCs, and no one can prophesy exact conversion rates.

The good client understands the risks and intricacies involved in fighting for profitability in a PPC account and is willing to (with excellent, and ongoing communication) adjust expectations and goals based on how the account is actually performing. This doesn't mean the account should always be kept open if profitability is not reached. *But, beware of the prospect who assigns an arbitrary deadline to the agency and holds their feet to the fire without being willing to learn from the agency if things change in the account.*

**Statement #4: "I need you to get back to me ASAP." or "You'll find we move pretty quickly around here." or "I know it's the weekend, but I need an answer today."**

I expect pushback on this one, but hear me out. In targeting this statement, I'm *not* discussing an account in which a client had their agency leave unexpectedly by breaking their contract, or an in-house employee left in a huff yesterday, or actual emergency scenarios.

Though, let me pushback on that pushback since, often, even emergencies can be indicative of poor original planning (how locked down was the contract you signed with the previous agency? Did the employee leave in a huff because your management is terrible and thus you have bigger problems than your unmanaged PPC account?). Even then, these are the exceptions, not the rule to these type of statements from my experience (I'm curious to learn from your experience on this one, BTW).

My primary concern here is that the individual demanding specific timing is (#1) showing signs of being the type of client who will always prioritize all of their questions as emergency status (#2) treating their agency partner as an employee rather than a partner.

#1 above is an issue because the number of times something in an account is *actually* an emergency is so minute, to be laughable. Thus so, the decision to find and hire a new agency is one that should be well-thought-out and researched. I much prefer to deal with a prospect who is willing to take things slowly in the beginning to ensure we are a good fit, rather than someone who "just needs to dive in right away, and by the way what is your lowest offer, we are ready to sign now, HURRY." I think this stems from a valuable lesson I learned from my parents while growing up, and that is, if someone pressures you into a hurried "deal" situation, it will 99 times out of 100 be something you didn't actually need or want anyway. *Let's all take the time to stop and think about a partnership potentially impacting the next years of our business lives.*

#2 above is an issue because the prospect is revealing they don't have a realistic view of the relationship they will have with an agency. If they want someone who they will have eight hours a day, who will have to pull every report for them, and who will jump with no pushback whenever they ask anything of them, then they need to hire an employee rather than an agency. One of the reasons an agency can be a smarter decision for certain clients in certain price ranges is because it offers them expert knowledge, or a team of experts, at a price that avoids the additional employee costs associated with an actual employee.

Put frankly, *beware of the prospect who is in a emergency-state rush to get started, as it often reveals a surface layer of deeper, problematic behaviors or philosophies.*

**Statement #5: "We've tried a lot of other agencies, but just haven't found what we're looking for yet."**

Ah yes, the wild and elusive "agency-hopper". Qualifications aside (sure there are some who have legitimately been burned by multiple agencies), this statement usually causes warning bells to ding all over my mind (and from talk around Social Media, I'm not the only one). As the PPC industry has begun to mature, it has become apparent that there is an evasive creature out there known as the "agency-hopper". This agency-hopper can be either timid and easily frightened, or ferocious and vengeful. Regardless of the type, both creaturely behaviors are dangerous to agencies as they jump from agency to agency, trying to find the perfect one, always frustrated and never satisfied.

The reason the agency-hopper is so dangerous to partnerships is because they tend to never find fault within their own methods or business. It is always the vendor's fault. Profitability wasn't achieved because the vendor failed in some way. Communication wasn't the best it could have been because the vendor failed. The timing of the moon's phases were out of sync because the vendor didn't answer my call. Time to find someone who will.

While some vendors are legitimately to blame for many things, at some point after the agency body count servicing the same client continues to rise, one begins to wonder if there is not more to the puzzle than simply the fact that this poor helpless client can't find a decent agency (but maybe someday? Maybe this next time?).

As a sidenote here to other agencies, one way to sniff out whether this is a legitimate prospect, or whether you are on the phone with the dreaded agency-hopper, is to learn the names of the previous agencies. If those agencies tend to all be well-regarded and reputable types around the web, then it's possible you are talking to an agency-hopper. *Beware of the prospect who is unwilling to consider their failings, but consistently blames it on their vendor and continues to look for a Superman to save the day.*

### Statement #6: The "INTERRUPTING COW"

This is a personal pet peeve of mine and since this is my (long) chapter, I get to add it in. This statement to be aware of is less of a statement, and more of a habit. When you were a kid, did you ever tell this Knock-Knock Joke?

Sarcastic Adult: "Knock-knock."

Unsuspecting Kid: "Who's there?"

SA: "Interrupting cow."

UK: "Interrupting cow, wh—"

SA: "MOOOOOOOOOOO" (bonus points for annoying volume).

In terms of agency speak, this is the person who won't let you finish your flipping sentences while on the prospecting calls! You may not notice it once or twice, but if it happens regularly over a call, I happen to think this is a red flag.

Here's why: someone who constantly interrupts you during your meet and greet is often revealing ego issues, and even more specifically, revealing deeper issues of who they see as the true king of this upcoming partnership here (hint: it's not you). When I am looking for a client, I am looking for someone who will treat ZATO as a trusted partner, not someone who refuses to even let us finish our sentences. *Beware of a prospect who does not value your input, right from the beginning.*

**Statement #7: "We can't afford your fees, but would you consider some sort of share in revenue?"**

See also "We don't actually have enough money scraped together to make this thing work, but we'd like to sink you with us."

Ok, maybe that was a little harsh (though, not too harsh). I realize everyone has to start somewhere, but what I've discovered is that promises of massive growth explosion rarely ever happen, and you may find yourself doing a lot of free (or undercharged) work for an account that will never take off. In the meantime, you still have your own mouth(s) to feed and bill(s) to pay.

As I alluded to in my opening salvo on this one, there is a very real concern here that the client is not financially stable enough to handle the inevitable ups and downs with marketing. You know who will get blamed in those downtimes, right? Hint: startup founders rarely blame themselves.

As an aside, this statement is different than an agency working out some sort of bonus structure as an incentive for proven, profitable work. Clients who say "how can I pay you well, and then reward you for doing an even better job" are not the type I'm referring to in this section. It is the client whose starting mindset is "how can I get the most work possible for the least amount paid out since I don't really have any cash on me" that concerns me. *Beware of the prospect who wants you to bear the primary risk of their business idea.*

**Statement #8: "PPC isn't complicated, I could do it I just don't have the time."**

Last but not least, we have to wrestle with the trickiest of all statements. This one is tricky, because I've never actually heard anyone explicitly utter the first part of it, but it comes through in a million ways. The short of it is that you are dealing with some-one (probably a business owner) who doesn't understand the intricacies of search and who believes it's really not that difficult when it comes down to it.

This directly impacts the level of respect they have for you in strategic decisions and/or what they are willing to pay. It can reveal an arrogance that will poison your future dealings with this client. I have found the best clients to work with are the ones who understand that they have value in their industry knowledge, and we have value in our PPC knowledge. This allows us both to strive to work together using each other's strengths.

Partnering with a person who downplays your understanding of PPC and how it fits into the broader scope of marketing as specialized is setting you up for many future conversations in which you will have to either (1) constantly defend your actions in an account or (2) constantly communicate around non-essential account intricacies that the client thinks are important and therefore demands an explanation. They simply don't trust you, and maintaining relationships that are not built on trust is exhausting.

I have had to ask this of a client before when we were approaching a relationship precipice, but if they genuinely do not trust or respect our expertise, then why did they hire us in the first place?! If you find clients who respect you, ask good questions at times, but overall remain confident in their decision to hire you, it will be exponentially easier to build and grow their accounts since you are working together in confidence for the good of their businesses. *Beware the prospect who does not recognize the complexities of PPC and your expertise in it.*

◆ ◆ ◆

So, there is my confession of what I watch for in client calls and in the prospecting process. Obviously, you don't always get things right. Sometimes you have suspicions about a certain client and they turn into a great relationship. Sometimes you don't see the red flags until three months into your relationship. It happens, but if you strive to build the right client base, you will find more stability in employee management, process, communication, and even your own mental health!

# CHAPTER 16 - IN CONCLUSION

*You Can Go Home Now... We're Done*

There you have it, now you know everything possible there is to know about PPC and digital marketing! The depths have been plumbed, and you will go from here with no need to learn more, ever again.

I kid, I kid. Don't stop learning! Keep learning about PPC, keep learning about marketing, and take that leap to go solo or become the Paid Search expert in your company. I hope this book has truly been helpful in getting you to think (remember, that was our goal when we first started out), and I look forward to connecting with you online to learn from you.

Connect with @PPCKirk to continue the conversation on Twitter or LinkedIn.

ZATO can be found at https://zatomarketing.com.

*May the auctions be ever in your favor.*

[1]Aaron Levy, "What You Think You Know About Your Customers' Persona is Wrong," blog post, 2015, *Acquisio Blog*, accessed 7 July, 2020, https://www.acquisio.com/blog/agency/what-you-think-you-know-about-your-customers-persona-is-wrong/.

[2] Ginny Marvin, "Google's Search Terms Move Will Make Millions in Ad Spend Invisible to Advertisers," blog post, 2020, *Search Engine Land*, accessed 24 September 2020, https://searchengine-land.com/googles-search-terms-move-will-make-millions-in-ad-spend-invisible-to-advertisers-340182.

[3] Emily Stewart, "Lawmakers Seem Confused About What Facebook Does – And How to Fix It," blog post, 2018, *Vox*, accessed 24 September 2020, https://www.vox.com/policy-and-polit-ics/2018/4/10/17222062/mark-zuckerberg-testimony-graham-facebook-regulations.

[4] Scott M Lewis, "Who Actually Owns Your Data," blog post, 2018, *Winning Technologies*, accessed 24 September 2020, https://winningtech.com/who-actually-owns-your-data/.

[5] Todd Spangler, "Facebook to Pay $40 Million to Settle Claims It Inflated Video Viewing Data," blog post, 2019, *Variety*, accessed 24 September 2020, https://variety.com/2019/digital/news/facebook-settlement-video-advertising-lawsuit-40-mil-lion-1203361133/.

[6] Google, "Payment methods & terms of service finder," *Google*, accessed 24 September 2020, https://payments.google.com/u/0/paymentsinfofinder?hostOrigin=
aHR0cHM6Ly9wYXltZW50cy5nb29n-
bGUuY29tOjQ0OTE.&sri=-21.

[7] Google, "Google, Inc. Standard Terms and Condi-

tions for Advertising," *Google*, accessed 24 September 2020, https://static.googleusercontent.com/media/www.google.com/en//ads/terms.pdf.

[8] Kirk Williams, "The One About Search Term Obfuscation & Google Edicts," LinkedIn article, 2020, *LinkedIn,* accessed 24 September 2020, https://www.linkedin.com/pulse/one-search-term-obfuscation-google-edicts-kirk-williams/.

[9] Google, "Google third-party policy," *Google*, accessed 24 September 2020, https://support.google.com/adspolicy/answer/6086450?hl=en.

[10] Sarah Sluis, "Google GM Sissie Hsiao Is Planning For The Next 'Jump Forward'," blog post, 2020, *Ad Exchanger,* accessed 7 July 2020, https://www.adexchanger.com/platforms/google-gm-sissie-hsiao-is-planning-for-the-next-jump-forward/.

[11] Kirk Williams, "Should Smart Shopping Include More Data? My Rebuttal to The Rebuttal – Part 6: The ZATO Guide to Google Smart Shopping Campaigns," blog post, 2019, *The ZATO Blog*, accessed 7 July 2020, https://zatomarketing.com/blog/should-smart-shopping-include-more-data-my-rebuttal-to-the-rebuttal-part-6-the-zato-guide-to-google-smart-shopping-campaigns/.

[12] Martin Röttgerding, "Debunking Ad Testing Part 1: Statistical Significance," blog post, 2018, *PPC Epiphany Blog*, accessed 7 July 2020, https://www.ppc-epiphany.com/2018/10/23/debunking-ad-testing-part-1-statistical-significance/.

[13] Joey Bridges, "How to Prepare For the Upcoming Changes of Google Enhanced Campaigns," blog post, 2013, *Search Engine Journal*, accessed 9 July 2020, https://www.searchenginejournal.com/how-to-prepare-for-the-upcoming-changes-of-google-enhanced-campaigns/60462/.

[14] Frederick Vallaeys, *Digital Marketing in an AI World: Future-proofing Your PPC Agency*, (Modern Marketing Masters, 2019), ac-

cessed 9 October 2020, https://www.amazon.com/Digital-Marketing-AI-World-Futureproofing-ebook/dp/B07QNMKK2L/ref=sr_1_1?dchild=1&keywords=fred+vallaeys&qid=1596333641&sr=8-1.

[15] Jesse Frederik and Maurits Martijn, "The New Dot Com Bubble is Here: It's Called Online Advertising," blog post, 2019, *The Correspondent*, accessed 21 August 2020, https://thecorrespondent.com/100/the-new-dot-com-bubble-is-here-its-called-online-advertising/13228924500-22d5fd24.

[16] Claude C Hopkins, *Scientific Advertising*, (Phoenix: Carl Galletti, 2008, 2017), accessed 8 September 2020, https://www.scientificadvertising.com/ScientificAdvertising.pdf.

[17] Kirk Williams, "All of My PPC Memes (So Far)," blog post, 2015, *The ZATO Blog*, accessed 9 October 2020, https://zatomarketing.com/blog/ppc-memes/.

[18] C.S. Lewis, *Mere Christianity,* (San Francisco: HarperOne, 2015).

[19] Timothy Keller, *The Reason for God,* (Westminster: Penguin Books, 2009).

# APPENDIX - THE STORY BEHIND THE BOOK

*While editing the final drafts of this book (huge thanks to my mother-in-law, Cindy Allen, for her proofreading skills), it hit me one evening that it may be helpful to include an appendix as a sort of mini-autobiography. I am somewhat hesitant to write a brief synopsis of my life that brought me to this point, as I see the temptation to think too highly of myself at times. While certainly we can delight in achievements and be thankful for them, a proper humility and awareness of our limitations is important.*

I decided to proceed with this Appendix for two reasons.

First, who we are directly relates into how we see the world. In other words, if this is a book of philosophical thinking about the world of PPC, it's probably going to be even more beneficial for you, the reader, to be aware of the backstory of the author so you can identify any potential biases I may have.

Second, I want to write this as somewhat of an inspiration. If I can do it, you can do it, too. I mean it when I say that. As you are about to see, I began PPC (and an agency) with zero connections and experience and believe that is something that anyone can do as well. I am not saying it is easy, or that I did not have other privileges to which some may not have access. I just want to encourage you to keep going.

# The Early Years

I was born in Minneapolis, Minnesota, to a Baptist pastor and his wife in the frigid month of January in 1985. Don't worry, I won't spend time on my childhood, other than to say that I had a blessed upbringing with loving parents, a roof over my head, and no fear of going hungry. Of course, later I would learn that my parents did experience some of those financial concerns, which is why we were blessed to have a connection to my grandparents' farm, from where much of our food came. I didn't realize this when I was growing up, but enjoying Grandpa and Grandma's garden and grass-fed beef wasn't simply an additional pleasure; at times, it filled a legitimate need for my family.

Though I was a blissfully ignorant child who had gifts to open on Christmas Day and enjoyed fun, rare surprise visits to McDonalds for happy meals, we really didn't have much money, but I didn't know that. My parents were focused more on serving others than they were on building a world empire of finances, and I am thankful for that experience growing up. I believe it helped teach me how earning money for the sake of having money is a poor focus. We were certainly happy without gobs of it lying around, and some wise saving and thriftiness ensured that we had plenty of toys with which to play.

Of course, the problem with that from a business perspective is that I didn't really have any concept of entrepreneurship or how to make money. Not only that, but I attended college and seminary with the objective of being a full-time pastor. I did not take a single business course of any kind, even though I have roughly 20 years of schooling behind me.

I say all that because I have heard stories of friends who began agencies with a good deal of capital, MBAs, family examples and training, or even just deep connections in the business community already. I had no training or knowledge base to begin with, and at times it shows. There are times I'm embarrassed to admit how little I know. At a conference a few years back, I remember jokingly, but shamefully, admitting to John Gagnon of Microsoft and a few other speakers (I think Aaron Levy and Elizabeth Marsten were there, too) that I did not know how to run an Excel pivot table. They were floored.

I note all this because what I did successfully was to find my advantage and lean into that, and that is easily something you can do in your own life as well. I found my advantage in specifically two ways.

First, I found that I could write. I could think through an argument, distill it into a structure, and then write it out quickly. Thank you, grad-level courses, for that one! In my first year of seminary, I took a course in which I calculated that each student wrote over 100 pages of material for that single class alone!

I didn't really know that my writing ability was a unique benefit until I talked to a speaker friend at a conference one year. This guy is a fantastic marketer and a great speaker. He knows his business and is very successful. We started talking about writing, and he noted how long it took him to write a single blog post and that he just didn't care for writing. I was surprised, as I hadn't realized that was an advantage I had in the market. I began to lean into that and churn out content. I wrote for PPCHero, I started writing for Search Engine Land, Moz, the Microsoft Ads blog, and Search Engine Journal. This writing is part of what introduced me to people like Ginny Marvin (previously with Search Engine Land), who was also connected to SMX Conferences, as well as the awesome Hanapin Marketing people who run the PPCHero blog and HeroConf.

Second, I found a group of like-minded PPCers on Twitter who valued connection, and I began to engage with them and build relationships. I spent HOURS on Twitter back in the day. I met people who are dear friends to me (some of whom have written reviews for this book; thank you, again!). I discovered that it was easy to complain about the Platforms too much as a group, so I did my best to try to keep conversations more positive with things like goofy memes, even as I was trying to add value in shared PPC knowledge. Ironically, making memes was a big part of how I began to get more followers on Twitter. People wanted to learn, but they also wanted their lives to be a little less drab, and at that time, memes on Twitter to PPCers were doing it. Who knew?! Psst, you can see some of those goofy old memes on my website to this day.

I included the above because I want to challenge you to consider your talents, skills, and privileges and how you can lean into them more. By the way, as a side note, I don't see "privilege" as inherently a bad word. It's something of which we need to be aware and by which we need to be humbled. For instance, I recognize how privileged I am to be born into a white, middle class, American home in the twentieth century. In terms of all the people who have ever lived in all of the world, I won the lottery through no action of my own. I'm not embarrassed by that, but I am humbled and thankful, and I want to use my unearned privilege to help others who don't have that.

You may not have the ability to write, but you may know SQL and, therefore, be able to think through a way to add that into your service offerings in a way I never could. You may have a business education, which will help you avoid many of the mistakes I have made, and you can leap-frog me in growth simply because you avoid money and time pits based on your education. You may have a great business network or access to capital.

On the flip side, you may have been born into an upbringing significantly less privileged than my own. In that case, just the fact that you're slogging your way through some horrifically boring business book means you are getting after it already. That's amazing, and you may have learned things growing up in this different setting that make you exponentially wiser in being able to quickly read people to close a business deal… or whatever else your upbringing might have taught you that you perhaps don't even know yet can be a strength.

USE IT. Identify and lean into your strengths.

We have all been given some sort of pros and cons, but we are so often inclined to think too much about our cons. I could list so many cons I have. I make decisions far too emotionally at times, and I have highs and lows that impact my ability to work as well as I can or lead as well as I would like. I make beginner mistakes in business because I don't have the training or experience to see what a freshman business student would avoid. Be realistic with your cons so you can grow out of them for sure, but lean into your pros and build your personal brand and business around your strengths! If I can do it, you can certainly do it, too.

## Our 2020

Let's get to 2020. When the pandemic and its impact hit in earnest in the US, it was the least impactful thing to hit my wife and me in the year… and that's not because it didn't impact us.

A few years ago we purchased a home that was a perfect fit for us both; it was our home through and through as it fit our styles and personalities. We loved it… only to find out a year later that it was in a subdivision in town where improper soil investigation (and/or resolutions to the revealed problems) had been done by the entities in charge of building this particular subdivision. Our house (along with dozens of others) began to experience significant foundation damage, and we had to go through two years of a heartbreaking process of working through what to do. Foundation issues are not covered by homeowner's insurance, and a lot depends on the state and city regulations as to what the original builder and/or developer are responsible to pay for damage such as ours.

Fast forward to January 2020, when we decided, after seeking much wise counsel, that it was best to sell our home at a major loss by fully disclosing everything and getting out. We took a $221K loss. Did I mention foundation issues are a big, expensive deal? We began to pack and gear up for an unexpected move, while we tried to figure out how we were going to lose $221K we didn't have. All of this happened as we began to hear of the alarming reports that China and Milan were burning from COVID-19. At least it couldn't get worse, right?

### It Got Worse.

During this time, my wife and I had discovered we were pregnant, and we took some delight in the new life begun in her as we packed up our home and sold our vehicles so we could eliminate as much debt as possible for our upcoming period of life (I miss my bright yellow FJ Cruiser that could drive anywhere).

Unfortunately, a week after we announced our pregnancy on Facebook, we received the terrible news that we had lost the baby. Of course, there are many things that go into the amazing miracle and complexity that is growing a living person inside of you... but both my wife and I believe the stress of that season was a key reason for the baby's death. We (especially my wife) were exhausted and heartbroken.

One month later, we gathered friends and family and moved into our storage unit and in-laws' home... the day before the governor of Montana locked down everything due to COVID-19 concerns. Our family of seven moved into the basement of my in-laws' home (again, if you're counting!) for the next three months until we were able to get into our rental (another silver lining story for another time) as we began to now pay off the six figure loan we had to borrow just to sell our broken home.

While it was a little packed in their home, I am very thankful for where we were as COVID lockdowns hit. My in-laws have an entire acre of property in Montana, so the kids were still able to play outside while we were locked down. I realize not everyone had that capability, so we were very thankful for the ability to kick our five children outside so the adults did not go stir-crazy!

A few months later, we packed up again, moved out of the storage unit and into our rental house, where we will remain until our lawsuit pays off our loan, or until we pay off our loan (much more slowly).

During all this, I was wrestling with the possibility that the pandemic would harm ZATO in a devastating way (it didn't and hasn't, though we had no idea in the beginning of the lockdowns if it would), as well as continue to service clients, write blog posts, appear on webinars, and basically do work as normal. It was exhausting. Props to my ZATO team. What an amazing group of people, as they pitched in and helped do extra when I was having a particularly rough day here and there. We experienced (to my knowledge) no negative impact from my personal issues on our clients even though I jokingly, but seriously, would refer to my personal life as "being in shambles" during that period.

Why do I bring up this potentially awkward peek into my personal life? Three reasons:

> (1) Truthfully, some of it is just to journal and write out my feelings. I process by writing. So, thanks for letting me journal to you.

> (2) This was an incredibly difficult time, but my wife and I believe that everything happens in our lives for a purpose, orchestrated by a powerful God who demonstrated His love for us by sending His Son to receive our just judgement for us. We are also incredibly blessed and thankful for the

many gifts of grace God has given us. This is a core aspect of our lives, and I would be negligent in leaving it out of an Appendix about our current situation. I would encourage you to investigate these truths if you are currently in a difficult place, searching for answers. If interested in learning more, I would suggest reading the *Gospel of John*, in the Bible, then <u>Mere Christianity</u> by C.S. Lewis[18] and <u>The Reason for God</u>, by Tim Keller[19], or you can always email me at kirk@zatomarketing.com.

(3) Finally, I want to give you hope. 2020 has been hard on everybody in different ways. There are ways the pandemic was much harder on others than it was for me hidden in little Montana. Heck, I got to publish a book in 2020, and that is something that has been on my bucket list virtually my entire life. I'm hanging onto that win for at least a few months!

Whatever is going on for you right now, you can get through it. Keep it up! Don't give up! You got this; I'm cheering for you.

A huge thank you for finishing my book, I do wish you the best in your life and ventures and let's make sure to connect on LinkedIn or Twitter in the near future.

# ABOUT THE AUTHOR

## Kirk Williams

 Kirk is the owner of ZATO, his micro-agency focused solely on Paid Search Advertising, and has been working in Digital Marketing since 2009. He is on the board of the Paid Search Association, and was named one of the Top 25 Most Influential PPCers in the world by PPC Hero from 2016-2020 primarily because of his PPC writing for various industry publications. Pre-COVID, he was an international conference speaker training PPCers on all things Paid Search (especially Shopping Ads). Kirk currently resides in Billings, MT with his wife, 5 children, Trek bikes, Taylor guitar, books, and little sleep.

Connect with @PPCKirk to continue the conversation on Twitter or LinkedIn.

ZATO can be found at https://zatomarketing.com.

Made in the USA
Las Vegas, NV
04 December 2020